# HEYER SOCIETY

### Essays on the Literary Genius
### of Georgette Heyer

## EDITED BY RACHEL HYLAND

Overlord Publishing
overlordpublishing.com

1 2 3 4 5 6 7 8 9 10

*For Janga.*

*"A remarkable woman, a benevolent contributor to the gaiety of nations. All English-speaking countries, I think, are grateful to this wonderful wit, this highly-principled and extraordinary woman whose world will never, never stale."*

– Stephen Fry, Georgette Heyer's Blue Plaque Unveiling Wimbledon, June 5, 2015

Also from Overlord Publishing

*Buffy the Vampire Slayer, Season Eight: Reviewed*
*Geek Versus Geek*
*The Grand Tour: A Georgette Heyer Travel Guide*
*Project Film Geek: 1929*
*Project Film Geek: 1930s*
*Reading Heyer: The Black Moth*
*Reading Heyer: Powder and Patch*
*Undercovers: Reviewed*
*The White Queen: Reviewed*
*YA Novels: Reviewed*

# CONTENTS

## APPENDICES

# FOREWORD

I was intrigued and delighted when I was invited to contribute to an anthology of essays on Georgette Heyer. It seemed a timely addition to the growing number of academic articles, theses and conferences on Heyer, as well as an appropriate marker for the decisive shift in attitude to Heyer's novels over the past twenty years. Though it is nearly a century since she published her first novel and almost forty-five years since her death, Heyer's books have gone on selling (more than a million sold in the last ten years alone), she has been deemed a Classic Author by the British Library Service and, in 2015, Georgette Heyer was awarded a prestigious English Heritage Blue Plaque. Consequently, those who have previously dismissed her novels as sentimental trash have been compelled to reconsider and perhaps even read them.

*Heyer Society – The Literary Genius of Georgette Heyer* offers a cornucopia of reflections, reactions, analyses, homages, criticisms and critiques of both the writer and her work. It is a book for fans but also for those who have yet to dip their toe into the Heyer universe. For some the appellation "genius" may seem too great a claim for an author perceived by many as a woman writing for women, but for those in the know her stylish prose, flawless syntax and ironic wit lift her books far above the ordinary. Georgette Heyer is one of those rare authors who can make me laugh out loud and for more than three decades she has been one of my favorite re-reads and the author whose books I turn to not merely for pleasure and inspiration but also for comfort in times of struggle and distress.

I am not alone in this. As generations of readers around the world will attest, Georgette Heyer is the perfect panacea for times of trouble. A. S. Byatt described her novels as "honourable escape" and Lady Ellenborough declared her the "only reading for a hospital bed." It is a testament to the quality of Heyer's writing that well into the 21st century she continues to be read. For those who know her books this is not surprising, for her readers revel in her characters and plots, her imbroglio endings, her mastery of period dialogue and in her effortless distillation of meticulous historical detail into her stories.

The two dozen essays in this collection offer readers still more reasons as to why Heyer is such an enduring writer. Among them are essays on Jane Austen's influence on Heyer, Heyer's influence on contemporary Regency, paranormal and science-fiction authors, Heyer's heroes, analyses of her suppressed novels, an appreciation of her wit and humor, life lessons learned from Heyer novels, cousins in Heyer, a look at some of the problems arising from Heyer's cultural bigotry, sex in Heyer, Heyer in film and the lasting impact of Georgette Heyer's novels on many modern writers.

Heyer once wrote that, "Most of my works would die with me, I fear; but one or two might continue selling for a while." The passage of time has proved her fear unfounded and today fifty-one of Georgette Heyer's fifty-six books are still in print and continue to sell in large numbers and multiple languages around the world. Her fans are legion and include men and women of all ages and nationalities.

*Heyer Society – The Literary Genius of Georgette Heyer* is a fun and feisty tribute to an author whose remarkable literary legacy may outlast us all.


*Jennifer Kloester,*
*Geelong, 2018*

# INTRODUCTION

I know it's pronounced "Hay-er." Or even "Hare," if you're particularly plummy. But to me, it will always be "High-er," because I grew up with that pronunciation, courtesy of my mother, who doubtless learned it at the knee of her own. Or perhaps it's like that anonymous meme that has been doing the rounds of social media for the past few years, and – unlike many of its ilk – rings so true: "Never make fun of someone if they mispronounce a word. It means they learned it by reading." We Hylands have long been mispronouncing Heyer, because we learnt it by reading, not by hearing – ever, *ever* hearing – about her.

Which is actually why this collection now exists. Alone of authors who have revolutionized fiction as we know it, Georgette Heyer remains the province of we happy few lucky enough to find her, through whatever circuitous route we did so, and thence immerse ourselves in her work. She is almost a cult figure, strange in a writer of such natural, unstoppable aplomb, still in print after almost a century. People know how to pronounce Pepys and Proust, even if they have never read their works (and most probably haven't). They can tell you all about Albert Camus and Annie Proulx. Certainly, the Brontës get their diaeresis recognized. These names are oft-heard, not only among the halls of the intelligentsia, but along the winding roads of pop culture referentiality—even if the young reader starts out saying "Peppies" and "Came-us," eventually "Peeps" and "Cam-oo" will catch up with them.

But Heyer, like the inimitable P.G. Wodehouse – a similarly, though less, unsung hero of the written word – is a name one could go a whole lifetime without hearing spoken aloud, and thus pronounce incorrectly forever. (It's "Wood-house," by the way.) That cannot stand.

This is not to say that Heyer does not have many millions of adherents the world over. Her work still sells, and sells in impressively large quantities; every day, new readers become evangelists as they merrily immerse themselves in her wondrous worlds. But take a random sampling of say, a hundred people. Perhaps the same hundred they poll on any given episode of *Family Feud*. And ask them, have you heard of Jane Austen? Yes. Agatha Christie? Of course. Georgette Heyer? Um… who? Survey says no. But Heyer undoubtedly belongs in such hallowed company, and deserves name recognition far wider than has thus far been achieved. A lack of film or television adaptation undoubtedly has much to do with this tragic oversight; something addressed (by, er, me) in this collection.

I'll not deny, of course, that in some ways I love the fact that Heyer's genius is something of a secret to the world at large. Who doesn't like being in the know, part of an exclusive order of enthusiasts who are just that little bit smug at their intimate acquaintance with a hidden, brilliant gem? It's like discovering an artist before they win an Alternative Music Grammy – though an artist that has been beloved for decades, and actually isn't that alternative at all (cf. David Bowie, in 2017).

The twenty-plus essayists herein are among an elite cadre of dedicated aficionados who not only know Heyer's early work – saw the show, bought the T-shirt – but have delved in depth into her entire catalogue, and have metaphorically followed her on every world tour. From scholars and acknowledged experts in the Heyerian field; to Regency authors inspired by Heyer's vision; to bloggers and fans with unique takes on her glorious creations; *Heyer Society* is not only a play on words – depending on how you pronounce it, of course – but also notes that we are among the privileged, the proud, who know and love and properly appreciate her novels – most of which are set in "Society," as well.

So however you say it, our title is also our mission statement, either as a pun that would utterly confuse poor darling Ferdy Fakenham, or as a testament to the glittering milieu in which our author so spectacularly laid many a scene, or, indeed, as a callout to likeminded souls everywhere.

Join us, won't you?

*Rachel Hyland*
*Melbourne, 2018*

# 1.

# GEORGETTE HEYER'S LITERARY GENIUS
# BY JENNIFER KLOESTER

In 2021 it will be one hundred years since Georgette Heyer, aged just nineteen, published her first novel. *The Black Moth* is a swashbuckling romance that owes something of its origin to the bestselling novels of Alexandre Dumas, Stanley Weyman and Baroness Orczy. Originally devised as a serial story when Heyer was seventeen to entertain her convalescent brother, *The Black Moth* is surprisingly accomplished for such a young author. The story of disgraced earl turned highwayman, Jack Carstares, the cast contains several characters whose nature and behavior are convincingly depicted. Lady Lavinia, in particular, is instantly recognizable as a spoilt, selfish narcissist whose demands on her guilt-ridden husband create a crisis in their marriage, and yet the teenage Heyer gives her a self-awareness and eventual contrition to make Lavinia complex and remarkably true to life. Despite her youth, in her very first novel Heyer demonstrated a surprising degree of insight into human nature: her characters evolve, their observations are frequently perceptive and their conversations are natural and intelligent. Unsurprisingly, *The Black Moth* is still in print.

For the first twenty-five years of her writing career, Heyer wrote novels in several different genres, including serious historical fiction, swashbuckling adventures, historical comedies of manners, contemporary fiction and detective fiction. By 1944 she had discovered that her forte lay in writing ironic comedies set in the English Regency period of 1811-1820. These were the novels that best pleased her and which she wrote with the greatest facility; they are also the novels that have won her five generations of readers. It is no small thing to write over fifty books, to sell in excess of thirty million copies and to still be a bestseller more than forty years after one's death, but Heyer wrote novels that can be read repeatedly with no diminution of pleasure. As with many a classic book, her novels change and grow with the reader: there is always something new to be discovered – some aspect of the story or characters that only come into clear focus with experience and maturity. This is but one element of her writing that has ensured Heyer's longevity. Only a small percentage of authors write books that outlive them, but Heyer is one of the few of her literary generation still read *en masse* in the 21st century.

Heyer's remarkable success owes much to her literary heritage and her mastery of prose. Her father, George Heyer (for whom she was named), was a vital influence in her formative years, for it was from him that Heyer developed her love of the great writers. She did not attend formal school until the age of thirteen but benefitted instead from being taught by her parents at home. Her mother Sylvia was an accomplished musician and a graduate of the Royal College of Music. A loving and attentive parent, she encouraged her baby daughter's early learning. Heyer's father was a Cambridge Classics graduate with a keen sense of humor and an acute ear for language. He spoke idiomatic French, could recite whole chapters of Dickens by heart and had a passion for the theatre. He was also a minor poet with several of his poems published in *Punch* and the *Pall Mall Gazette*; as adults he and Georgette would read, edit and assess each other's work. Her relationship with her father would prove pivotal in Heyer's writing life.

She was a voracious reader raised on a rich literary diet of Horace, Aristophanes, Chaucer, Shakespeare, the Renaissance poets and playwrights, Defoe, Austen, Thackeray, the Brontës, Dumas, Dickens and a wide range of 19th- and early 20th-century novelists, historians and poets. Shakespeare was a particular influence and Heyer immersed herself in his works and became adept at playing her family's favorite Shakespeare trivia game, wherein players would have to identify the Act and scene from a line of dialogue or the line of dialogue from the Act and scene. Shakespeare, Austen and Dickens would prove hugely influential in Heyer's writing life, and it is not surprising that her best books – the Georgians and the Regencies – owe much in their devising to these great writers. Heyer took pleasure, both conscious and unconscious, in paying homage in her writing to her favorite authors: using Shakespearean quotations as book titles and frequently taking Shakespearean, Austenian and Dickensian characters and plots as the starting-point for her own plots and characters.

Jane Austen was her favorite novelist and her books are the ones Heyer said she would choose if stranded on a desert island. It was from Austen that she learned the art of ironic comedy and of closely observing one's fellow beings. Heyer delighted in taking characters, their foibles and fortes, from life and writing them into her novels. Austen also proved a valuable source of Regency words and phrases, and Heyer frequently used Austenesque language in her stories. Such was her admiration of Austen, however, that in her own novels Heyer would deliberately use Austen's words differently – as a gesture of authorial respect for her literary mentor. For example, where Austen writes in *Pride and Prejudice* that Caroline Bingley "paid off every arrear of civility," in *Sylvester* Heyer deliberately uses the phrase in the opposite way and writes of Mrs. Orde who "paid off every arrear of a debt of rancour."

From Dickens Heyer imbibed the lessons of memorable character creation. Her novels are replete with superbly drawn, unforgettable characters who live for her readers. People like Jonathon Chawleigh in *A Civil Contract*, one of Heyer's brilliant literary achievements. A comic character par excellence, the hugely wealthy yet vulgar Chawleigh is the perfect foil for the quiet, upper-class hero whose financial straits force him into marriage with an heiress – Chawleigh's plain, practical daughter, Jenny. The story is both humorous and poignant and it is a measure of Heyer's genius that she is able to write both comedy and tragedy within a single scene. There is real life here and high emotion and the reader is a treated to a masterful display of the writer's craft as we watch Jenny and Adam struggle in their relationship which, despite many obstacles, gradually grows and develops over time.

From her earliest novels, Heyer wrote with an extraordinary ease, creating stories and characters that, from the very first sentence, engaged her readers. Her 1926 novel, *These Old Shades*, written when Heyer was just twenty-one, became an instant bestseller and more than ninety years later it remains a perennial favorite. From the opening line she draws her reader into the story, creating an atmosphere of intrigue and introducing us to one of her most enduring creations: his grace, the Duke of Avon:

*A gentleman was strolling down a side street in Paris, on his
way back from the house of one Madame de Verchoureux. He
walked very mincingly, for the red heels of his shoes were very
high. A long purple cloak, rose-lined, hung from his shoulders
and was allowed to fall carelessly back from his dress,
revealing a full-skirted coat of purple satin, heavily laced with
gold; a waistcoat of flowered silk; faultless small clothes; and
a lavish sprinkling of jewels on his cravat and breast. A three-
cornered hat, point-edged, was set upon his powdered wig, and
in his hand he carried a long beribboned cane. It was little
enough protection against footpads, and although a light dress
sword hung at his side its hilt was lost in the folds of his cloak,
not quickly to be found. At this late hour, and in this deserted
street, it was the height of foolhardiness to walk unattended
and flaunting jewels, but the gentleman seemed unaware of his
recklessness. He proceeded languidly on his way, glancing
neither to left nor to right, apparently heedless of possible
danger.*

This is Heyer's "sequel" to *The Black Moth* in which a facsimile
of the villain of that first book becomes the cynical hero of what
would eventually be her sixth novel. Though written only two years
after *The Black Moth*, *These Old Shades* shows how much the author
has matured: her characters have more depth, the dialogue is more
sophisticated and the story offers a surprisingly ruthless ending for
the villain. There is romance here, of course, but it is an unlikely
romance between an older, world-weary man and a feisty younger
woman. In Léonie, Heyer created an entirely new kind of romantic
heroine – one who was courageous, enterprising and outspoken. It is
in this book that Heyer begins to turn the traditional romance on its
head.

Six years after *These Old Shades*, Heyer published its sequel,
*Devil's Cub*, in which she plays further games with romantic
stereotypes and creates her first anti-heroine in strait-laced and
principled Mary Challoner. Part of Heyer's genius lay in her ability to
pinpoint with deadly accuracy her readers' expectations of 'what
happens next' before skillfully inverting the scene to create comedy
instead of melodrama. *Devil's Cub* is replete with many of the
traditional romantic elements: a dashing hero, a spirited heroine,
elopement, abduction, flirtation, seduction, mismatched lovers, even

a mysterious man in black, but none of these follow the usual trajectory – instead of raping the heroine, the hero is forced to hand her a bowl in which to vomit; instead of submitting to his advances, she shoots him; rather than casting her off, he demands she marry him; and, so far from falling into his arms, she sets out to make her own way in the world. The story is so skillfully told and infused with such ironic wit that it is transformed from the potentially banal into compelling prose. As Professor Diana Wallace points out, it is Heyer's "command of form and style that enabled her particular brand of elegant romantic comedy."[1]

Like Elizabeth Bennet in *Pride and Prejudice*, Heyer loved a laugh and she found her greatest satisfaction in writing clever comedies of manners and books replete with ironic humor. During the first twenty-five years of her writing career, she became a master of comic timing, witty dialogue and the imbroglio ending. The imbroglio ending was a particular specialty and the finales of books like *The Grand Sophy*, *Cotillion*, *Sylvester*, and *The Unknown Ajax* are masterpieces of plotting. Heyer once wrote, "My style is really a mixture of Johnson & Austen – & what I rely on is a certain gift for the farcical."[2] Professor Wallace suggests that, "she plays ironic intertextual games with the conventions of the form she herself had established."[3] This is true. Heyer knew the rules of romance – girl meets boy, something keeps them apart, the obstacles are overcome and they are united – and she conformed to these rules – up to a point. Heyer did not believe in sentimentality or that true love was some breathless, deathless emotion guaranteed to make one overlook a lover's faults. Instead, Heyer's ideal romance was the "marriage of true minds"[4] for she was, as Carmen Callil has said, "a stern realist."[5] In her novels, Heyer reserved the sweet, sentimental romances for her minor characters and delighted in poking fun at them – at their pretensions, their delusions and conceits. It is Heyer's major

---

[1] Diana Wallace, "Georgette Heyer," *The Literary Encyclopedia*, 5 November 2005.
[2] Georgette Heyer to Max Reinhardt, letter to Reinhardt as CEO of The Bodley Head, 20 July 1963.
[3] Diana Wallace, "Georgette Heyer," *The Literary Encyclopedia*, 5 November 2005.
[4] William Shakespeare, Sonnet 116.
[5] Carmen Callil in Carmen Callil & Colm Toibin, *The Modern Library: the 200 Best Novels in English Since 1950*, Picador, 1999.

characters who experience what she thought of as real love and her lasting relationships are reserved for those who become friends before they become lovers. As Frederica discovers in her eponymous novel:

> *"Is it like* that*? Being in love? You see I never was in love, so I don't know … It has always seemed to me that if one falls in love with any gentleman one becomes instantly blind to his faults. But I am* not *blind to your faults, and I do* not *think that everything you do or say is right! Only – Is it being – not very* comfortable *– and cross – and not quite happy when you aren't there?"*
> *"That, my darling," said his lordship, taking her ruthlessly into his arms, "is* exactly *what it is!"*

Frequently, Heyer uses one or more of her minor characters to throw her main protagonists into sharp relief. For example, in *The Grand Sophy* the Adonis-like but ineffectual would-be poet, Augustus Fawnhope, wanders through the novel oblivious to most of what is going on around him. Yet his presence in scene after scene provides the impetus for other characters' actions and reactions. For all his ineptness, in Heyer's hands, Fawnhope proves a remarkably effective provocateur. As Eric Selinger, in his essay on the poet- or poetry-novel notes:

> *Although* The Grand Sophy *aims to melt in your mouth like the best English trifle, Heyer takes her roles as dessert chef quite seriously, and her sure hand with Fawnhope shows throughout. His poetic self-involvement, for example, may be a familiar caricature, but Heyer uses it deftly to underscore the novel's concern with 'fit conversation,' in Milton's fine old phrase, as both proof and the embodiment of love. The more Sophy and Charles square off, like the Spencer Tracy and Katherine Hepburn of 1816, the better they suit each other, and that suitability plays out as a shared mastery of language.*[6]

---

[6] Eric Selinger, "Foils, Fakers, Monsters and Makers," *Parnassus Poetry in Review*, Vol. 29, 2006.

Language was vitally important to Heyer, and her Regency dialogue is one of the hallmarks of her writing which renders her, as the late Colleen McCullough described her, "inimitable."[7]

Regency argot came as naturally to Heyer as her own 20th-century English. Words like "bosky," "jug-bitten" and "foxed" meaning drunk, or "bouncer," "faradiddle" and "clanker" meaning lies; to have no money and thus be "in the basket," "at low ebb" or "dished" or to have plenty and be "well-breeched," "swimming in lard" or "plump in the pocket" – these sorts of phrases were all meat to the delectable literary dish of Heyer's contriving. When the Earl of Wroxford tells his son in *Charity Girl*, "You're a skitterbrain, Sir! A slibberslabber here-and-thereian," we may find the individual words unfamiliar but we instantly understand their intent and know they are not a compliment.

No one writes Regency dialogue like Georgette Heyer, and the best of the contemporary band of Regency authors openly acknowledge her influence on their writing. Heyer's vocabulary was astounding and she had a remarkable ear for rhythm and cadence so that even her most obscure language flows. Today, her novels are practically primers on how to incorporate unfamiliar historical language into accessible dialogue for a modern audience. She read widely, mining archaic dictionaries and early 19th century novels, magazines, letters, journals, and histories for words and phrases that would lend authenticity to her characters' conversation. In addition to the regularly-used 'high-society pieties of the *ton*,' she also used boxing slang, thieves cant, the upper-class slang that fashionable young men culled from their grooms and coachmen, the language of costume and carriages, and, as Laurie E. Osborne has noted, various "complex, often-unmarked appropriations of Shakespeare." The depth and breadth of her research enabled her to create dialogue that is at once energetic, alive and utterly convincing. As British author and actor Stephen Fry astutely observed, "It's her language I think that most admirers of Georgette Heyer relish."[8]

Heyer's dialogue not only set the tone of the era in which her Georgian and Regency novels are located, it also revealed character,

---

[7] In conversation with the author, book-signing, Geelong, 2009.
[8] Stephen Fry, Blue Plaque Unveiling, 103 Woodside, Wimbledon, 5 June 2015.

so that even the most minor figures, though they may only appear in a book once, *live* for her readers. Sir Timothy Wainfleet in *The Foundling* – despite occupying only a page or two – is wholly realized when he tells Lord Lionel:

> *"I suppose I must have liked you once," he said plaintively. "I like very few people nowadays; in fact, the number of persons whom I cordially dislike increases almost hourly."*

And in *The Convenient Marriage*, Miss Charlotte Winwood becomes instantly familiar in just a few pious sentences:

> *"Will he come?" demanded Charlotte. "What irremediable harm may not Horry's impropriety have wrought? We must ask ourselves, will Lord Rule desire to ally himself with a Family one of whose members has shown herself so dead to all feelings of Modesty and female Reserve?"*

While in *Bath Tangle*, even so unimportant a personage as the hero's steward, Mr. Wilton, is rendered three-dimensional in the briefest of conversations:

> *"Oh, no, my lord. But, then, I have known you for a very long time, and have become quite accustomed to your fits of the sullens," said Mr Wilton reassuringly.*
>
> *Rotherham's eyes gleamed appreciation. "Wilton, are you* never *out of temper?"*
>
> *"In my position, my lord, one is obliged to master one's ill-humour," said Mr Wilton.*

Such was her extraordinary ability to create convincing characters that among Heyer's minor characters are some so compelling that many readers wish she had a written a book just for them. Gideon Ware of *The Foundling* and Lord Legerwood of *Cotillion* are just two of these. Though Lord Legerwood has but a few scenes in the novel, he ranks among Heyer's most attractive men:

> *Lord Legerwood, in the act of raising his claret-glass to his lips, lowered it again, and regarded his son almost with awe. "These unsuspected depths, Frederick—! I have wronged you!"*

*"Oh, I don't know that, sir,' Freddy said modestly. 'I ain't clever, like Charlie, but I ain't such a sapskull as you think!"*

*"I have always known you could not be, my dear boy."*

As Professor Wallace has observed, while "Heyer's Regency is her own artificial invention it is her play with language that makes it both coherent and satisfying."[9]

Heyer's Regency world was a carefully constructed one, informed by the social and cultural mores of her own era, but based firmly on the historical record available to her at the time. She immersed herself in early 19th century sources and, though she was selective in her choice of material – focusing mainly on the upper class, her knowledge of the period and her ability to diffuse its culture, language, people, etiquette and ephemera into her novels was extraordinary. Those who read her Regency novels will often speak of their profound sense of actually *being there*: world-building at its best. She wrote with such nuance and subtlety, such irony and wit, that it is only through multiple readings that the reader can fully appreciate the layers of meaning in her stories. As her first biographer, Jane Aiken Hodge noted, "There's something so sane about these books – they say something quite profound about the relationships between men and women, and there's a strong vein of ironic intelligence running through."[10]

Heyer's genius was multifaceted. It lay in the creation of her characters, in her understanding of human nature, in the clever plots, often with imbroglio endings, and in her dialogue. These elements combined allowed her to create a world so believable that readers around the world continue to immerse themselves in it. As Stephen Fry explained: "She so subsumed herself in the age and became such a mistress of its language, its modalities, and its architecture, its locations, its locales. The milieu was just hers and nobody came

---

[9] Diana Wallace, "Georgette Heyer," *The Literary Encyclopedia*, 5 November 2005.
[10] Jane Aiken Hodge, *The Private World of Georgette Heyer*, The Bodley Head, 1984.

close."[11] Despite her selective approach to history and the inevitable influence of her own 20th century culture and experience on her world-building, Heyer's 19th century Regency world *feels* real. As *Time* magazine put it, in 1964: "… as with the late William Faulkner, you don't buy a book, you buy a world. If it suits you, you settle down forever."[12]

*~HS~*

**Jennifer Kloester** first read Georgette Heyer's novels while living in the jungle in Papua New Guinea and re-read them while living in the desert in Bahrain. In 2004, she completed a Doctorate on Georgette Heyer and her Regency Novels. Since then she has written extensively about Heyer and the Regency and has given writing workshops and public presentations in the UK, USA, Australia and New Zealand. She is the author of *Georgette Heyer's Regency World* and *Georgette Heyer: Biography of a Bestseller*. Jennifer also writes fiction; her novel *Jane Austen's Ghost* will be available in 2019.

---

[11] Stephen Fry, interviewed by Sara-Mae Tuson, Fable Gazers Podcast Company, September 2017 for Season 2 series: "Heyer Today" – due 2019.
[12] *Time* Magazine, 21 February 1964.

# 2.

# A MOST EXCELLENT INFLUENCE – GEORGETTE HEYER'S DEBT TO JANE AUSTEN

## BY SUSANNAH FULLERTON

Hookham's Library was in Bond Street. Established by bookseller and publisher, Thomas Hookham, it offered the latest works by Anne Radcliffe and Clara Reeve, amongst others, and was one of the two largest circulating libraries in Regency London. Judith Taverner of *Regency Buck* goes there one day to return a copy of Maria Edgeworth's *Tales of Fashionable Life* and to find something else to read. As she browses, she is suddenly greeted by her cousin, Mr. Bernard Taverner, and she shares with him her amusement at the book she has just picked up from the "new publications" on offer:

> *"Tell me, have you read this novel? I have just picked it at random from the shelf. I don't know who wrote it, but do, my dear cousin, read where I have quite by accident opened the volume!" He looked over her shoulder. Her finger pointed to a line. While he read she watched him, smiling, to see what effect the words must produce on him.*
>
> "I am glad of it. He seems a most gentleman-like man; and I think, Elinor, I may congratulate you on the prospect of a very respectable establishment in life."
>
> "Me, brother! What do you mean?"
>
> "He likes you. I observed him narrowly, and am convinced of it. What is the amount of his fortune?"
>
> "I believe about two thousand a year."
>
> "Two thousand a year?" and then working himself up to a pitch of enthusiastic generosity, he added: "Elinor, I wish with all my heart it were twice as much for your sake."

*A laugh assured Miss Taverner that this passage had struck her cousin just as she believed it must. She said, closing the volume: "Surely the writer of that must possess a most lively mind? I am determined to take this book. It seems all to be written about ordinary people, and, do you know, I am quite tired of Sicilians and Italian Counts who behave in such a very odd way.* Sense and Sensibility! *Well, after* Midnight Bells *and* Horrid Mysteries *that has a pleasant ring, don't you agree?"*

Georgette Heyer knew all too well, when she wrote that passage, that the author of *Sense and Sensibility* had a very lively mind indeed. In this delightful scene in *Regency Buck* she pays tribute to Jane Austen, her favorite novelist.

Any modern reader wishing to learn more about the life and era of Jane Austen can turn to a plethora of books on the subject. Georgette Heyer was not so fortunate. James Edward Austen-Leigh's *Memoir* of his aunt had been published, and Chapman's invaluable editions of Austen's novels and letters became available in the 1920s and 30s. She could also have read Constance Hill's *Jane Austen: Her Homes and Her Friends*, but there was little other biographical information which could tell Georgette Heyer more detail about the novelist whose works influenced her more than any other. However, she made the most of what she had, and echoes from Austen's novels and letters pervade Heyer's fiction. For any reader who loves both novelists, it is fun seeking out such connections. As one reviewer of *Friday's Child* noted, "The author has read Jane Austen to advantage, but so she should."[13]

We see in Jennifer Kloesters' *Georgette Heyer: Biography of a Bestseller* that the two women had quite a lot in common. Both began telling stories to entertain their siblings, both adored their fathers and lost them early, both treasured their privacy and did not court fame, neither suffered fools easily, both were meticulous craftswomen who knew their own limitations when it came to choosing plots and characters, and each displayed intelligent humor and an exact and unsentimental attention to detail in their writing.

---

[13] *The Saturday Review*, 23 February 1946.

*Sense and Sensibility* is a novel about sisters, one with sense and the other with sensibility (though the lines of demarcation are not always exactly drawn). *Frederica* gives us the rational, practical and sensible sister, who knows what can be afforded and what cannot (like Elinor Dashwood), while her beautiful sister Charis is weepy, sentimental and impulsive (just like Marianne Dashwood). Other sister pairs in Heyer reflect Austen's contrasts, such as Mary and Sophia Challoner of *Devil's Cub*, and Horatia and Elizabeth Winwood of *The Convenient Marriage*. All these sisters end up married. Austen shows in her first published novel, and in all her subsequent fiction, that marriage is more than simply a matter of two people falling in love. Economic, social and family issues, shared values and complementary personalities must also play a part in courtship and in the eventual happiness of the married pair. Second attachments can succeed, and handsome young men can prove to be rotters. Heyer learned these lessons in *Sense and Sensibility* and examined them in her own books.

*Northanger Abbey*, only published after Jane Austen's death, was her parody of the hugely popular Gothic genre. Heyer's *The Reluctant Widow* also plays with the Gothic, beginning on a cold, dark night, with a heroine taken to a gloomy, rambling house where she meets a dying man and an overbearing "villain" (who of course turns out to be the hero). Catherine Morland dreams of being abducted, but Hero in *Friday's Child* is forcibly swept into a carriage in a way that would meet all Catherine's wildest imaginings. Again, Heyer, like Austen, parodies fictional abductions, by having completely the wrong man force Hero into the carriage, while in *Devil's Cub* Vidal unknowingly drives off on a dark night with the wrong woman in his carriage – a hilarious twist on the Gothic trope. And in *Faro's Daughter* someone is locked in a cellar – not the heroine kidnapped by a dastardly villain, but the hero Max Ravenscar, who has been knocked on the head at the order of Deb Grantham. Gothic devices are mocked, subverted and parodied by both authors. One of Heyer's least popular novels, *Cousin Kate*, could perhaps have been improved had it played with Gothic conventions more than it does. Serious violence, mental disturbance, secrets and attempts at enforced marriage can all be found within its pages, without the leavening note of humor that Heyer usually adds to her fiction.

Detective writer P.D. James once described *Pride and Prejudice* as "Mills and Boon, written by a genius." Certainly, its plot of "boy meets girl, boy and girl misunderstand each other, boy and girl end happily" is pure category romance, but Jane Austen's much earlier version adds such psychological complexity, such richness of language, and such depth of perception to events that her novels are lifted into the realm of genius.

Heyer often uses this standard romantic plot herself, borrowing from Austen, but adding her own delightful twists. Arabella overhears Mr. Beaumaris slight her, just as Elizabeth Bennet has to listen to Darcy describing her as only "tolerable" at a ball. In both cases, the heroine's pride and prejudice are awakened, and these misunderstandings have to be worked through as a result. *Sylvester* is as proud as Mr. Darcy, his proposal to Phoebe as inept and gauche. The Duke has lessons to learn and could well say, with Mr. Darcy, "by you I was properly humbled." What fun it is watching both men learn from such spirited heroines. But it is not only men who learn – young women have also to understand themselves and their world. Half way through *Pride and Prejudice*, Elizabeth Bennet lays down Darcy's letter, seeing all too vividly the blindness of her past behavior. She states: "Until this moment I never knew myself." Judith Taverner has a similar moment during her ill-considered carriage race in *Regency Buck*. Heyer's novels are full of "learning courtships": Sherry must learn from Hero to think of others in *Friday's Child*; Mr. Beaumaris must learn about the awful conditions of chimney sweeps and stray dogs in *Arabella*; and Freddy Standen of *Cotillion* has to learn that love can come into one's life in unexpected ways. Couples who spar in seeming dislike, just like Elizabeth and Darcy, are in many of Heyer's books – *Bath Tangle, Black Sheep, Lady of Quality, The Grand Sophy* and *The Unknown Ajax* see heroines accused of being shrews, and heroes called overbearing and impossible.

Mr. Darcy first finds himself thinking seriously of Elizabeth because of her very fine eyes. Heyer echoes this often in her books – Anthea, Annis, Venetia, Penelope and a score of others have noteworthy, beautiful eyes (usually "cool grey ones") which reveal their delightful personalities and attract their lovers, just as Elizabeth's eyes draw Darcy to her.

Elizabeth Bennet "dearly loves to laugh," as did her creator. Jane Austen once confessed "I could not sit seriously down to write a serious Romance under any other motive than to save my life; & if it were indispensable for me to keep it up & never relax into laughing at myself or at other people, I am sure I should be hung before I had finished the first chapter." All Austen's heroines laugh (even Fanny Price – once!), and Heyer's heroines have a lively appreciation of the ridiculous: "Ancilla burst out laughing…" (*The Nonesuch*); "Miss Thane's eyes twinkled" (*The Talisman Ring*); "Pen's eyes lit with sudden laughter" (*The Corinthian*); "I wish you won't make me laugh just as I am drinking soup" (*Venetia*); while "gurgles of laughter", "her lips twitched", and "irrepressible smiles" are common phrases throughout Heyer.

*Mansfield Park* is a novel in which cousins marry. *The Unknown Ajax* gives readers the same result, as does *The Grand Sophy* (and surely in that novel the Marquesa is another Lady Bertram, with her ability to sleep through everything?). But *Mansfield Park* also contains adultery, dangerous illness, and marital unhappiness – all of which can also be found in Heyer. Heyer shows, just as did Jane Austen, that the penalty paid by men for immoral behavior is very different from the heavy price paid by women. Jenny Chawleigh of *A Civil Contract* read *Mansfield Park* after her marriage to Adam, perhaps finding in its pages consolation in the idea that a man's first love can be replaced by a stronger and deeper love second time around. Miles Calverleigh in *Black Sheep* has made his fortune in the West Indies, just like Sir Thomas Bertram, and the issue of absentee landlords is common to both novels. Dr. Grant's obsession with food and wine is mirrored by that of Sir Bonamy Ripple in *False Colours*, and by Sir Hugh Thane in *The Talisman Ring*; Tom Bertram's addiction to gaming finds a parallel with *The Convenient Marriage*'s Horatia Winwood, and the many young bloods who lose money dicing, playing cards or betting on horse races. Fanny Price is taken in by relatives and is not always comfortable in her adopted home. Neither is Kitty Charing of *Cotillion* happy in Mr. Penicuik's draughty Arnside House, or Hero Wantage with her relatives the Bagshots, or Cousin Kate when she ends up with her aunt Lady

Broome. Finding a happy home is an important theme for both novelists. Echoes from *Mansfield Park* are scattered throughout Heyer's fiction.

But my absolute favorite of Heyer's tributes to Jane Austen is her reincarnation of Pug. Lady Bertram is devoted to her pug, though she seems not even to be entirely sure what sex her dog is. Jane Austen uses this lap dog to devastatingly illustrate the vacuous, selfish character of its mistress who cares more for her pet than she does for her children. Heyer does the same when she puts a pug into *Friday's Child* with fabulous comic results. Lady Saltash is the owner of a fat, stertorous pug and poor Hero must assist in his care – she has to brush the obese animal's coat and take him for short walks. It is on one of these walks that she is abducted by Mr. Tarleton, who mistakenly believes that she wants to be whisked to Gretna Green and does not realize that she is already married. As Pug is on the end of the leash when Hero is hauled into the carriage, Pug naturally follows her into the vehicle. And he then becomes a confounded nuisance. When Sherry arrives to rescue her, he is horrified: "No, dash it, Kitten! I don't mind Gil's canary – at least, I do, but I can bear it – but I'll be hanged if I'll have an overfed little brute like that in my house! If you want a dog, I'll give you one, but I warn you, it won't be a pug!" He goes on to question his wife as to what she "could possibly have wanted with a dog when you were eloping?" Neither pug is given a name, both dogs play minor roles but achieve a great deal when it comes to illustration of character, and both provide marvelous comedy.

Emma Woodhouse is a managing female, because she does not have enough to do. Sophia Stanton-Lacy is, like Emma, an expert manager. As one character tells her, "When I last saw you, you were engaged in arranging in the most ruthless fashion the affairs of the most bewildered family of Belgians I have yet encountered." Sophy enters the Rivenhall household like a whirlwind, sorts out its financial and romantic problems, organizes a ball, manipulates her father, and arranges social life for all her newly met relations. I believe that Heyer found models for many of her other characters in the pages of Austen's masterpiece, *Emma*. Miss Bates, who never stops talking, was surely in Heyer's mind when she created Maria Farlow of *Lady of Quality*, with her inexhaustible flow of "…

nothing-sayings," while Mr. Woodhouse's hypochondria must have influenced the many vaporish, health-obsessed characters to be found in Heyer – Lady Ombersley of *The Grand* Sophy is one such character who greatly enjoys her "indifferent health." That wonderful social climber Mrs. Elton with her "*caro sposo*" and her "Knightley" is the model for memorable snobs and social mushrooms in Heyer's Regency novels – Mrs. Challoner, who has "visions of entering the Polite World" and snubbing her city relatives, is one, while pushy Mrs. Broughty, "voluble, and wonderfully assured" is another. And surely dim-witted Harriet Smith is the model of Belinda of *The Foundling* – both girls fall for stolid young farmers, both adore pretty clothes, and both are very easily swayed by a stronger personality. And Mr. Elton's awkward proposal in a carriage, a terribly funny scene in which Heyer must have delighted, was surely in her mind when she described Mr. Tarleton proposing in a carriage to a woman already married (*Friday's Child*).

Georgette Heyer also had fun with *Persuasion*, Austen's tale of lost love and second chances. In *Bath Tangle* we think we are getting another two versions of Anne Elliot's romance – Serena was engaged to Ivo, Marquis of Rotherham, but it was broken off. But Serena was also once in love with a handsome military man who had no fortune, so her father "could not countenance the match." He went away, but suddenly returns into her life and all is set for Serena to find happiness with her handsome soldier. But Heyer delighted in playing with our familiarity with Austen, so she challenges our expectations, and has Major Kirkby fall in love with Serena's stepmother instead.

Elsewhere, Abigail Wendover of *Black Sheep* is, like Anne, an older heroine, fairly certain that she will never marry. So is Annis Wychwood of *Lady of Quality*. Like Anne, both women have relations who want to control them; like Anne, Annis and Abigail have belated chances of marital happiness.

Both Jane Austen and Georgette Heyer wrote about young women of marriageable age who enter the marriage market, frequently at a disadvantage in some way or another. Both authors center their fiction on a romantic relationship, but then proceed to de-center it by the use of comic irony and by un-romanticizing the institution of marriage. Love or lust are not enough. Their heroes and heroines must have something else in common – intelligence, humor, compassion, tenderness of heart. While both novelists avoid the vulgar, they do touch on some of the scandalous aspects of the Regency age – illegitimate children, sexual misconduct, duels, money-lending, planned elopements and abductions. Both are excellent commentators on the effects of money (what W.H. Auden called in Jane Austen "the amorous effects of brass"[14]) and show how marriage prospects are heavily influenced by a want of fortune. Both analyze the effects of the unstable Regency era – Waterloo, enclosures, the madness of the King, a growing middle class, industrialization and political and rural poverty are some examples of this. Their heroines must depend on their own wits, integrity and insight into other people, while coping with unfit or absent parents, unkind guardians, loss of a home or income, and the attentions of seductive but unreliable young men. Heyer and Austen share an unerring sense of place, giving their characters just the right addresses to reveal their financial and social position, and moving them around the English countryside with accuracy of detail. Few authors knew with such exactitude what their perfect milieu was – Heyer occasionally strayed into detective fiction or other eras of history, but today is remembered and loved chiefly for her Regency romantic fiction.

While each author is inimitable in her own way, there is of course no novelist who can touch Jane Austen. Heyer never provides the psychological brilliance, the depth of characterization, and the sheer innovation that we find in the pages of Jane Austen. Heyer would have been the first to admit that her own genius was far inferior to that of her literary mentor. When she received a letter from a fan who claimed that she had just succeeded in "wading thru" *Pride and Prejudice* and concluded that it was a Heyer book "with a lot of unnecessary padding," she tore the letter to bits in disgust. Her reviewers might comment that her Regency novels were "good enough to fool any but the most puristic Janeite,"[15] but Heyer was a puristic Janeite herself and knew that her books were simply not in the same class.

---

[14] W. H. Auden, "Letter to Lord Byron," *Letters from Iceland,* 1937.
[15] Mary Fahnestock-Thomas, *Georgette Heyer: A Critical Retrospective*, Prinny World Press, 2001.

That said, Heyer can also offer us things we cannot find in Austen. Unlike Jane Austen, who was writing for a contemporary audience, Heyer provides far more historical detail, detail she often found in Austen's letters, such as minutiae of food, fashions, modes of transport and entertainments. Such detail is one of the charms of her novels. She gives us more Dukes and titled aristocrats than does Jane Austen, and most of us relish this entry into the world of the *haute ton*. She uses more slang than Austen, but what reader could object to such colorful phrases as "a trifle disguised," "barque of frailty," "'pon rep.," "dicked in the nob," "pitching the gammon" or "pulling caps"? Jane Austen chose names for her characters with care, but without flamboyance. Heyer, on the other hand, gives rein to her fancy and provides us with some marvelous names. Who could forget Sir Nugent Fotherby? Ivo, Marquis of Rotherham, a stormy character, has a name which could have escaped from a Brontë novel, while Augustus Fawnhope is exactly the right name for a wannabe poet. Heyer was brilliant at nomenclature.

Readers can rejoice in the differences, sigh with satisfaction when echoes of phrase and situation from Austen turn up in Heyer, and enter with huge pleasure the Regency world they described. It thrills me that one of my favorite novelists constantly echoes and pays tribute to my very favorite novelist. Jane Austen and Georgette Heyer are both "regular out and outers" and "high steppers" in the world of literature. I find them "complete to a shade" in every way that matters.

*~HS~*

**Susannah Fullerton**, OAM, FRSN, is the President of the Jane Austen Society of Australia, literary lecturer and tour leader, author of *Jane Austen and Crime, A Dance with Jane Austen, Happily Ever After: Celebrating Jane Austen's Pride and Prejudice* and *Jane & I: A Tale of Austen Addiction,* and co-editor of *Complete to a Shade: Georgette Heyer, A Celebration.*

# 3.

# FROM ARABELLA TO VENETIA – GROWING UP WITH HEYER'S HEROINES

## BY RACHEL HYLAND

From about the age of thirteen, after I had finally read all of them, my favorite novel by Georgette Heyer was, hands down, *Arabella*. (Full disclosure: I didn't get to the mysteries and contemporaries until much later.) This 1949 entry into the Heyerian canon gives us the spirited, tender-hearted Arabella Tallant, new in London and launched into Society with some fanfare, due to a rash declaration of fabulous wealth to one Mr. Beaumaris, whom she had overheard supposing her to be a fortune hunter, sight unseen.

Arabella's travails spoke to my adolescent self as did no other Heyer heroine's. Yes, partly it was because she's so young, just eighteen or so, which was close enough to my own age that it felt simultaneously very grown up yet wholly relatable. But Horry from *The Convenient Marriage*, Kitty from *Cotillion*, Pen from *Regency Buck* and certainly sixteen-year-old Hero from *Friday's Child* were all correspondingly youthful, their years not so very much more advanced than my own. Married Nell from *April Lady* has barely escaped from the schoolroom herself, and the same could be said of Léonie from *These Old Shades*, had she ever really been in one. And as for Juana from *The Spanish Bride,* she is just fourteen at the start of the novel, when she is all but forced into marriage with her Captain Harry. (It's based on a true story, Heyer was constrained by the realities of war brides and saving women on the battlefield from gang rape, and Harry seems to have been a good man who did the right thing. It's still… not okay.)

So why was Arabella so utterly appealing to me, over those many equally age-adjacent heroines?

A lot of it was due to the outlandish way in which she challenged the world-weary Mr. Beaumaris so valiantly. I thrilled at the way she stood up to him, even if she was wildly naïve in how she went about it, and I felt like it was something I might very well have done myself, in such a circumstance. But I think it was mostly due to her social activism, the way she saves that poor wretched climbing boy and then rescues the abused stray dog, these acts of charity unusual in the Heyer realm, in which most of our heroines are in no way malevolent, but neither are they exactly crusaders for reform. True, Arabella essentially abdicates her duty to these unfortunates once the much put-upon Mr. Beaumaris takes them in his charge, and it is through this that we see him fall under her spell as he is called to care about something more than his own comfort, but the very verve with which she tackles these projects, and the winning manner in which it all works out for the best, is pure teenage wish fulfillment, and I found it utterly entrancing.

And then! Even more wish fulfillment, as the much older, much more sophisticated, and – let us not forget – much richer Mr. Beaumaris forgives Arabella all her folly and follows her to her family's modest home in the country to declare his undying devotion. There are no social consequences to Arabella's impetuous claims of great wealth, or her scandalously planned elopement. There is no ostracism, nor embarrassment. This was especially pleasing to my teenage self, to whom the threat of public humiliation was possibly worse than any other psychic torture. (Not that, if I'm honest, too much has changed on that score.)

But that is definitely why *Venetia* snuck up on me as my new favorite Heyer, as I entered my twenties. *Venetia* was not a book in which public humiliation was out of the question. In fact, our heroine positively courts it, and I just could not understand her. How could she not care for Damerel's dire reputation? For her runaway mother's ostracism? For her own position in the world? To the then-me, Venetia seemed to me to be worse than even Phoebe from *Sylvester* and Serena from *Bath Tangle*—and, to a lesser extent, Abigail from *Black Sheep*. Because while Heyer thankfully never really hit us too hard with the social ruin in any of her books, those three were always among the hardest for me to reread, all that awkwardness and the worrisome feeling that our heroine could not possibly get out of the mire in which she had managed to entangle herself with her reputation intact. (Yet, somehow, I was fine with Robin and Prue's potential for devastating discovery in *The Masqueraders*. Huh.)

31

And *Venetia* I didn't reread at all until, embarking on a complete journey through all of Heyer's works about ten years after I had first discovered them, I decided I really had to give it another go, just for the sake of completeness.

And I fell completely in love.

Part of it was, I think, that having reread *Arabella* yet again, at the lofty age of twenty-one, its heroine was no longer such a paragon of all the virtues, but instead felt to me very immature and entitled, which wasn't a word people were using yet, but is the one that most fits my thoughts at the time. Part of it may even have been the freshness of *Venetia*, since I hadn't read it in ten years, and was not only seeing it anew but also through new eyes. But neither of these things fully explains the sudden change in my perceptions of this book. After all, ten years later I still loved Kitty and Hero and Pen. Ten years later, I still didn't love *Cousin Kate* and *The Reluctant Widow* and *False Colours*.

So what changed?

Partially, it was Lord Damerel. Damerel is in his late thirties, and his face is unprepossessing, and he is a rake and a scoundrel who has been selfish and careless with other peoples' lives and hearts. It is hard for a thirteen-year-old girl to find that kind of hero appealing, I think. And nor, indeed, should she. True, Justin, Duke of Avon is even older, and is possibly even more dastardly, than Damerel. But when Monseigneur wins the adoration of his young ward, and then adores her right back, it is an elaborate fairy tale treating with French royalty and baby switches and kidnapping plots that has little to do with our mundane world. When Damerel and Venetia become friends, and then become more, it all feels *real*. And that was perhaps more than I could cope with at the time.

This, I think, is because *Venetia* is Georgette Heyer's *sexiest* book, and I wasn't ready for it at thirteen. I still prefer Trad Regencies and Clean Contemporaries over their racier counterparts, anyway, and I always will, but what was evident in *Venetia* upon an adult reading was a simmering physical awareness between Damerel and Venetia that was simply beyond my ken as a younger reader, certainly well-versed in category romances of both the adult and teen school, but not yet fully awakened to the exquisite, agonizing joys of unresolved sexual tension. (*The X-Files* was still a couple of years away, back then.)

And then there's Lady Steeple.

Poor Lady Steeple. When first I read *Venetia*, all wide-eyed and full of righteous indignation, the idea that a woman could not want children, could abandon them to their fate with an inattentive father while she went gadding about Europe indulging her every whim, was such anathema that I found it hard to forgive Venetia for not being more outraged. Arabella would not have stood for such treatment. Arabella would have marched into that dressing room and demanded satisfaction, answers, and probably reparations for the whales killed in the making of Sir Lambert's creaking corsetry. But Venetia was just so very *nice* about it all. Teenage me did not get that at all.

Adult me found it to be one of the most touching scenes in all of Heyer.

The fact that Lady Steeple had never wanted children, had certainly not wanted to marry the much older, temperamental scholar that was Sir Francis Lanyon, but had done so to assuage parental, and societal, expectation is hard to ignore when you read this book from a feminist perspective. True, it's unnatural in a parent to disown their offspring, but what is Lady Steeple but an unnatural parent? Unwilling, certainly, and the fact that her opinion of her infant son, Aubrey, could be colored by such vacuous concerns as aesthetics surely calls into question her general fitness for motherhood. In another age, she might have had the luxury to choose childlessness. Back in 1818, when this tale was set – and, indeed, perhaps even in 1956, when it was written – given her class and education and status, she really didn't.

For Venetia to be hurt, yes, but also so understanding, so forgiving of this frailty in her long-absent mother... as a grown up, it is admirable. As a teenager full of angst and melodrama and anger at the world for no apparent reason, it was infuriating as hell. (Of course, one could be cynical and suggest that Venetia is so kind to the vain, silly mother who abandoned her because she wants a favor from her. But let's not.)

I honestly believe that I can chart the path of my growth as a person through my reactions to Heyer's novels. Reading *The Talisman Ring* as an adult, it is the humor-filled courtship of Tristram and Sarah that catches my enduring fancy, rather than the fiery adorableness of young lovers Eustacie and Ludovic, so appealing in my youth. Reading *The Nonesuch* as an adult, my focus is on the mature romance of the estimable Sir Waldo and erudite governess Ancilla Trent, rather than entering deeply into the petulant feelings of spoiled beauty Tiffany. Reading *Sprig Muslin* as an adult, I have little care for the ardent passions of runaway would-be bride Amanda, and instead cheer for Hester and Sir Gareth and their gentle Friends-to-Lovers Happily Ever After.

And reading *Arabella* as an adult – look, I still like it. I like it a lot. Arabella's feistiness, Mr. Beaumaris's (eventual) thoughtfulness, the rescued mutt Ulysses, even Tallant brother Bertram's financial woes, all are still an endless delight. But Venetia – and Hester, and Ancilla, and Sarah, not to mention Annis and Abigail and the wonder that is Frederica, et al. – now appeal to me far more as heroines than do their younger counterparts, because in their speaking eyes and their quirked lips and their clever ripostes and their gradual realizations of dawning love, they make sense to me in a way that Arabella and Kitty and Pen never can again.

Really, there is a Heyer heroine for almost every age, and taste, and temperament.

Which speaks to her genius. That she can give us so many different experiences within the very same pages, that she can appeal to us throughout our entire lives, that we can discover new depths in her works upon each new read through, and new favorites among books long-since read and reread *ad infinitum*—this is a rare gift in a writer of any genre, and one that cannot and should not be underestimated.

Somewhere between *Arabella* and *Venetia*, I grew up.

Somewhere in reading Georgette Heyer, I grew.

*~HS~*

# 4.

# THE HEYER PROBLEM – A HISTORY OF PRIVILEGE

## BY CAT SEBASTIAN

In historical romance, we have a Heyer problem. She did such a compelling job of worldbuilding that sometimes her version of early 19th century England seems more salient than actual historical fact. At its core, historical romance has been shaped in Heyer's image; the problem is that this image is fundamentally hostile to marginalized groups. The world she invented depends on massive quantities of privilege, leaving us with a genre that has privilege and hierarchy baked right into it. Georgette Heyer's Regency, populated largely by extremely wealthy, often titled, always pedigreed members of the British upper class, has been replicated in so many books it's taken on the force of reality; any deviation from Heyer's world is perceived as either implausible or inaccurate.

*The Grand Sophy* is the most obvious example: it's charming, it's witty, it's an absolute *tour de force* of everything most beloved about Heyer, from the grumpy hero to a frankly disturbing number of animals—until the scene with the money lender. Immediately the reader is forced to either abandon the book or accept that in this narrative Jewish people are only worthy of caricature and scorn. For a Jewish reader, this can only be alienating and marginalizing in the extreme; the book is loudly announcing that it is not for you. But it's also saying something else: this world of Heyer's belongs to a narrow group of people.

This alienation takes place on a lesser scale throughout all Heyer's work: in order to be carried along with the narrative, the reader is forced to accept the marginalization of any character who isn't an able-bodied member of the English upper class. To read Heyer, you would think that England was entirely white, secular, and uninterested in fighting injustice. You could be forgiven for assuming that the poor were ignorant and grasping, the middle class entirely composed of vulgar social climbers, that "foreigners" were lazy and dishonest, that people of color did not exist, that the chronically ill were often malingering, and queer people were either absent or reviled. There is nothing wrong with stories about the tiny segment of society that made up the *beau monde*—people have loved tales of glittering wealth and luxury since probably the dawn of time. But Heyer does more than focus her lens on members of the upper class: she actively disdains, belittles, and marginalizes anyone who falls outside that group.

The problem is that since Heyer's Regency has been reproduced so many times in modern historical romance, a story centering on a character outside Heyer's narrow world doesn't ring true to many readers. In the decades since Heyer more or less invented the genre, we've seen a broadening of Regency-set historical romance: main characters can be disabled (although their treatment may not be ideal), poor (as long as they end up reasonably rich by the end), and queer (although I can attest that there's a solid contingent of readers who find the notion of happy queer people to be wildly improbable before about 1980). People of color and non-Christians are still rare. In reality, England in the late Georgian era was a hotbed of political radicalism, increasing racial diversity, wide-spread education, and a thriving (although persecuted) queer subculture.

Basically, Heyer warped our notions of history, and she did it by doing such a good job of selling this world that she invented. Her world is just so compelling—people are clever, the dialogue is sparkling, and the happy ending restores order to the central couple and also the world. Sometimes I reread *Venetia* (which, despite my having spent the past five hundred words complaining about Georgette Heyer, is one of my favorite books in any genre) and it's so perfect that it's nothing short of incredible that anybody (including this writer) had the nerve to ever again set another book in the Regency *beau monde*. But the fact that we had precisely that nerve is what I'm writing about: there are thousands of books that are set in Heyer's reality rather than actual historical reality, which means that it has shaped reader expectations. So many readers of historical romance start with Austen, then find Heyer, then arrive at historical romance (this isn't the only pathway, or even necessarily the most common, but there's enough of a Heyer-to-romance pipeline for it to be an established pattern).

To borrow Georgette Heyer's world is to implicitly exclude huge swathes of people, but to throw it out would mean abandoning Regency-set romance entirely. Some writers have managed to tell stories in the spaces allowed by Heyer, quietly populating her world with diverse characters and infusing it with a less restrictive sensibility. Some writers, especially those who belong to the groups marginalized or ignored by Heyer, have worked to reclaim that time period, have subverted the tropes and themes we expect in a Regency-set romance. There are Jewish, Black, Asian, queer, disabled, and many other writers setting out to actively challenge the expectations that are fundamental to Heyer's work, redefining what a happy ending looks like and who deserves one. I'm not certain it's possible for Regency-set historical fiction to ever completely break free of Heyer's influence, and I don't think that's even a reasonable goal. But by being conscious of the few places where Heyer fell short, we can do a better job of respecting the people of the past and the present.

*~HS~*

**Cat Sebastian** writes steamy, upbeat historical romances. They usually take place in the Regency, generally have at least one LGBTQ+ main character, and always have happy endings. Cat lives in a swampy part of the South with her husband, three kids, and two dogs. Before her kids were born, she practiced law and taught high school and college writing. When she isn't reading or writing, she's doing crossword puzzles, bird-watching, and wondering where she put her coffee cup.

# 5.

# MARKS OF DISTINCTION – HEYER'S MARK I AND MARK II HEROES

## BY JANGA

Almost a century ago, Georgette Heyer created types of heroes so appealing to readers of historical romance fiction that they became prototypes for countless writers who followed. Rare indeed is the writer of historical romance novels who has not, directly or indirectly, copied or adapted Heyer's patterns.

Her Mark I heroes, a designation Heyer herself used, are descendants of Edward Rochester, hero of Charlotte Bronte's *Jane Eyre*.

Like Rochester, Heyer's Mark I heroes are dangerous and dissolute with scandalous reputations. Heyer's first biographer, Jane Aiken Hodge, herself an author of romance fiction, notes that Heyer described her Mark I heroes as "the brusque, savage sort with a foul temper." But Heyer was too good a writer to be bound by a formula, even one of her own devising, and her Mark I heroes evolved from Justin Alastair, the Duke of Avon (*These Old Shades*, 1926), who possesses the brusqueness, savagery, and foul temper of the original description, to Max Ravenscar (*Faro's Daughter*, 1941), who has some of Avon's savagery but lacks the more villainous qualities, to Lord Jasper Damerel (*Venetia*, 1956), whose rakish behavior is several degrees less disreputable than his reputation suggests.

### Justin Alastair, Duke of Avon, *These Old Shades*

When a teenaged Georgette Heyer wrote her first novel, the melodramatic *The Black Moth* (1921), to amuse her sick brother, she created her first Mark I, although in this case he is the villain. In fact, so steeped in infamy is the Duke of Andover that he has earned the nickname "Devil." He is selfish, cynical and amoral; nevertheless, there is something compellingly attractive about him. Predictably,

Andover's evil plans are foiled by the noble hero and this villain remains untamed and unredeemed.

When Heyer began *These Old Shades* a few years later, she used the Georgian setting of her first novel and adapted a number of its characters as well. Most notably, Devil Andover becomes Justin Alastair, the Duke of Avon, hero of the new novel. Avon has the coldness, the arrogance, the acerbity that characterized Andover. His seeming omnipotence coupled with his arrogant indifference to society's rules and his willingness to do what is necessary to achieve his ends led to his nickname, "Satanas."

But unlike Andover, Avon is redeemable because he is capable not merely of desire but of love. Transformed by his love for Léonie, a fiery-haired, cross-dressing urchin with an old soul and a fierce devotion to her Monseigneur, whom she views as her savior, Avon develops selflessness and a sense of honor. Avon buys "Léon" and at first, he views the gamin as a tool that will make possible his revenge against an old enemy. But as he grows to care for her, it is the crime which robbed her of her class, even her gender, that drives him. When she is restored to her rightful place, he is prepared to give her up because he thinks he doesn't deserve her. He confesses:

> *My reputation is damaged beyond repair...I come of vicious*
> *stock, and I have brought no honor to the name I bear. Do you*
> *know what men call me? I earned that nickname, Child. I have*
> *even been proud of it. To no woman have I been faithful;*
> *behind me lies scandal upon sordid scandal. . . . Infant, you*
> *are worthy of a better husband. I would give you a boy who*
> *might come to you with a clean heart, not one who was bred up*
> *in vice from his cradle.*

Avon's only friend Hugh Davenant predicts that Léonie will be Satanas's "salvation," and so she proves as Avon, without ever losing his arrogance and cynical edge with others, shows himself capable of tenderness and even humility with his beloved.

> *His Grace looked deep into her eyes, and then went down on*
> *one knee and raised her hand to his lips. "Little One," he said,*
> *very low, "since you will stoop to wed me, I pledge you my*
> *word that you shall not in the future have cause to regret it."*

Avon becomes the hero he has denied being.

## Max Ravenscar, *Faro's Daughter*

Even a superficial description of Max Ravenscar should make readers of 21st century historical romance novels aware of this character's prototypical qualities: he is in his mid-30s, an admired athlete and horseman, and, although unmarried, the head of his family, most of whom he endures with ill grace. His power, and he is very powerful, rests in his strength of will, in his great wealth, and in his unshakable conviction that he is in control. Not classically handsome, he is tall, dark, "with a good pair of legs," and "a lean, harsh-faced countenance with an uncompromising mouth and extremely hard gray eyes."

Like Avon, he is "a proud, disagreeable man" with manners that are "not conciliating." Like Avon, he manipulates people to achieve his own ends. Like Avon, he is supremely confident of his own judgment.

But Ravenscar has a humanness that is lacking in Avon until his feelings for Léonie begin to transform him. Ravenscar has a genuine affection for his younger cousin and ward, and his relationship with his half-sister is marked by an ease and a closeness quite different from the authoritative role Avon assumes toward his siblings. Ravenscar says that his sister "has always been in the habit of telling me things, and she sometimes even takes my advice."

Ravenscar also has a sense of humor; when our heroine, Deborah Grantham, asks how he can reasonably object to her using help to kidnap him since she could not possibly do so alone, he bursts into laughter. His relationship with her is nearer that of Fitzwilliam Darcy's with Elizabeth Bennet that to Avon's with Léonie. Rather than redeeming him, love will teach Ravenscar that appearances can be deceptive and that "laughing eyes" and a mind that holds his interest are more important than social standing in choosing the right wife. Yet even in his determination to marry the challenging, contradictory, high-spirited Deb, he remains arrogant and confident of his power within his world. When Deb reminds him of the social chasm between them, Ravenscar says, "I shall marry a wench out of a gaming-house with as much pomp and ceremony as I can contrive."

## Lord Jasper Damerel, *Venetia*

Damerel is the quintessential Regency rake. So scandalous is his behavior that it "was almost a social solecism to mention his name in polite company." While scarcely more than a boy, he ran away with a "married lady of title," an act that destroyed his future, broke his mother's heart, and caused his father to have a stroke—or so the *ton* insists. When Venetia Lanyon meets him for the first time, she observes his "careless elegance," "cynically bored" eyes, and "swashbuckling arrogance" and is reminded of Byron's Corsair: "There was a laughing devil in his sneer."

But as the two become friends, without denying his rakishness, she recognizes qualities in him that are at odds with the image he projects.

> *"I know you for a gamester, and a shocking rake, and a man of sadly unsteady character!—but I'm not so green that I don't recognize in you one virtue at least, and one quality."*
> *"What, is that all? How disappointing! What are they?"*
> *"A well-informed mind and a great deal of kindness,"* she said.

He also possesses a lively sense of humor, and, as with Ravenscar and Deb, Heyer uses the bond of laughter to show the attraction and growing intimacy between Venetia and Damerel. Like Avon, Damerel is convinced that his beloved is too innocent for a man of his experience. He sends her off to London and worthier suitors and finds solace in a bottle. It is the heroine who takes action when she finds out that her hero has been acting nobly when he rejected her.

In a conversation with her scandalous mother, Venetia makes clear why a rake, not a prince, is the man she dreams of:

> *"... you know what that Prince in the fairy-tale is like ma'am! Young, handsome, and virtuous! And probably a dead bore,"* she added thoughtfully.

> *"Well, my usurper is not very young, and not*
> *handsome, and certainly not virtuous: quite the reverse,*
> *in fact. On the other hand, he is not a bore."*

Her mother responds, "You have clearly fallen in love with a rake!"

So she has, and she clearly hopes that he will retain some of his rakish ways, promising that marriage will not mean the end of his orgies and other indulgences. It is Damerel who is insistent upon reform and determined that his bride not be ostracized by the *ton* he once scorned. His declaration shows him still feeling unworthy:

> *"You may regret this day: I could not! What I regret I can*
> *never undo, for the gods don't annihilate space, or time, or*
> *transform such a man as I am into one worthy to be your*
> *husband."*

For readers who encounter Heyer's heroes after reading countless historical romances, it is tempting to see in them well-worn conventions of the sub-genre. But Heyer was establishing conventions rather than following them. She began with a villainous rake who preyed on women and in subsequent books made him a hero transformed by his love for a woman and committed to protecting her even at the sacrifice of his own happiness.

Heyer's mark on the genre remains solid more than three-quarters of a century after her first creations, but her Mark I heroes are only half the story. The influence of her Mark II heroes is no less profound.

*The Black Moth* features not only the rough pattern of her Mark I heroes in its villain, but also a first draft of her Mark II heroes in its hero, Jack Carstares, Earl of Wyncham. Carstares possesses some of the Byronic qualities that are associated with the Mark I hero, but these characteristics in Carstares are a consequence of his circumstances, not of his character. He is forced into exile because he assumes the guilt that is his brother's. When he has the opportunity to kill Andover, he spares his life. Even in his role as highwayman, he remains chivalric and debonair, a man of honor with winning ways.

The Mark II heroes who follow Carstares remain essentially true to the pattern. Like Mark I heroes, they are often wealthy and well-dressed, but they lack the Mark I's arrogance and assumption of omnipotence. Genial, even-tempered, and well-liked, the Mark II hero is generally younger than the dangerous Mark I, and he has a greater respect for conventions. Heyer characterized her Mark II heroes as "suave," in opposition to the "savage." "Suave" in this description carries with it none of the pejorative connotations of insincerity and manipulation, but rather the less common meaning of affability, courtesy, and friendliness.

As with the Mark I heroes, Heyer never becomes formulaic but creates a variety of Mark II heroes who are more than they appear to be, ranging from Sir Anthony Fanshawe (*The Masqueraders*, 1928), who disguises his discernment and physical power behind a superficial indolence, to Anthony Verelst, Viscount Sheringham (*Friday's Child*, 1944), whose youthful blue-eyed fairness undercuts the Byronic pose he assumes, to the Honorable Frederick Standen (*Cotillion*, 1954), whose anti-heroism reverses all the heroic clichés.

### Sir Anthony Fanshawe, *The Masqueraders*

For readers conditioned to measuring heroes by Avon and company, Sir Anthony Fanshawe is an unlikely hero. From his first appearance, his size and his lethargy are stressed.

> *The large gentleman paused on the threshold and put up his quizzing glass, through which he blandly surveyed the room. He was a very large gentleman indeed, with magnificent shoulders and a fine leg. He seemed rather to fill the room; he had certainly a presence, and a personality. He wore a wig of plain brown and carried his hat under his arm. The hilt of his sword peeped out from between the folds of his great coat, but in his hand he held a cane.*

He has arrived to rescue heiress Letty Grayson from a rogue and from her own foolishness, but when he discovers her rescue has already been effected, he is more interested in his dinner than in the heiress. Robin mockingly refers to him as a "mammoth" and a "mountain," both terms perhaps suggesting a large creature lacking in quickness. But the narrator hints that Sir Anthony's looks are deceptive: "His hand was very white and finely shaped, but it looked to have some strength." The large gentleman's sleepy eyes are at times "alert," and while he is "a most respectable gentleman," lacking the dash and danger of a Mark I hero, he makes Prudence feel "all woman."

While Prue as Peter Merriot, and Robin as Kate Merriot are deceiving all of London with their disguises, Fanshawe sees through their deceptive clothing and carefully cultivated mannerisms. He even suspects their connection to the "old gentleman." Prue realizes that he "had very nearly the full sum of it." He sees danger "on all sides" and wants Prue out of the masqueraders' game, but he understands her loyalties and admires the qualities in her that enable her to carry out so successful a deception. He says to her: "I have nothing but pride in you. In your courage, and in the quick wits of you. I have never known so wonderful a woman." There is nothing indolent about him when he forces a duel on a man to prevent Prue as Peter Merriot from meeting said man, and he demonstrates his physical and mental quickness when he rescues Prue from the officials who have arrested Peter Merriot. And he meets the most essential requirement of a romantic hero, as Prue recognizes when she says to him, "You gave me the happy ending I never thought to have."

### Anthony Verelst, Viscount Sheringham, *Friday's Child*

Spoiled and self-indulgent, fashionable in dress and careless in attitude, Sherry Cunningham appears to be if not a full-fledged Mark I hero, at least a Mark I in training. But the key word here is appearance. Even the not particularly perceptive Isabella Milborne, the Incomparable, who rejects Sherry's marriage proposal, knows that his romantic looks are artful:

> *No he was not as handsome as poor Wrotham, whose dark stormy beauty troubled her dreams a little. Wrotham was a romantic figure, particularly when his black locks were dishevelled through his clutching them in despair. The Viscount's fair curls were dishevelled too, but there was nothing romantic about this, since the disorder was the result of careful combing.*

Even Sherry's rakish behavior is more youthful experimentation than committed lifestyle. Sherry is one of Heyer's youngest heroes, only 23. Heyer herself emphasized his youth in a description of the novel.

> *There is a certain young man who has appeared in several of my books—he was Cedric Brandon in* The Corinthian, *Viscount Winwood in* The Convenient Marriage—*and some others! And once I said idly that I would one day write a frivolous story about that young man. This is it. This time he is Viscount Sheringham (Sherry), the story begins with his runaway marriage to a very young lady whom he's known since childhood, and with whom he isn't the least in love. And the story is about all the circumstances which lead (a) to his partial reform and (b) to his falling in love with his wife (of course!).*

Like many of the young male characters to whom Heyer refers, Sherry wants to be a Mark I hero, but his youth, his inexperience, his amiability, even his fair coloring all serve to distance him from the dissolution and power of the Mark I. Sherry's marriage to Hero Wantage begins his journey toward maturity and self-understanding. Since she is a true innocent and even younger than he, her mistakes, most of them resulting from following Sherry's advice, force him to consider his choices more carefully. When she runs away, Sherry realizes that he loves her and that he can no longer be the impetuous youth he was before he assumed the responsibilities of marriage. Closing references to dogs and babies indicate that his responsibilities are likely to increase, as is his maturity.

### The Honorable Frederick Standen, *Cotillion*

Freddy Standen is the very antithesis of the heroic. He does share with many Heyer heroes an attention to fashion, but unlike Sir Richard Wyndham (*The Corinthian*) or Robert Beaumaris (*Arabella*), Freddy is defined by his sense of fashion and his knowledge of "all matters of social usage." The first description of him makes clear that from his "brown locks, carefully anointed with Russian oil, and cropped à la Titus" to his feet clad in "effulgent riding boots," Freddy is a very "Pink of the Ton." The white tops on his riding boots ally him with those like Beau Brummell (who introduced this fashion) that have no interest in the sweat and dirt associated with sporting activities.

Heyer includes in *Cotillion* two figures reminiscent of a Mark I hero. Reading the description of Freddy's cousin Jack, a reader might think she has just been introduced to the book's hero:

> *...a tall man whose air and bearing proclaimed the Corinthian. Coat, neckcloth, fobs, seals, and quizzing-glass, all belonged to the Dandy; but the shoulders setting off the coat so admirably, and the powerful thighs, hidden by satin knee-breeches, betrayed the Blood, the out-and-outer not to be beaten on any sporting suit. The face above the starched shirt-points was a handsome one, with a mouth as mocking as its owner's voice, and a pair of intensely blue eyes which laughed into Freddy's.*

It is Jack with whom Kitty Charing imagines herself in love. It is Jack whom their uncle intends to be his heir. It is Jack who is "if not a downright rake... certainly the most accomplished flirt in town." He has the reputation, the strength, the skills, the cutting tongue, and the arrogance of a Mark I hero. But Jack cares too much for himself and his own pleasures to fall in love.

The other heroic figure is Freddy's father, Lord Legerwood, a Mark II hero post-marriage and family. A "sportsman and a gentleman," he is a wealthy, handsome man who possesses "cool, well-bred manners . . . an air of decided fashion, too, and an occasionally satirical tongue." Somewhat tamed by many years of domesticity, he also has a twinkle in his eye, a decided affection for his wife, and a conviction that his eldest son is incapable of sustained thought.

Both men underestimate Freddy. Jack finds laughable the idea of Freddy as a threat to Jack's own plans, and Lord Legerwood doubts that Freddy has the mental capacity to bring off a deception. At first, Heyer does little to undercut the image of Freddy as an ineffective fribble. Not satisfied with the first impression of him as a Dandy lacking the intelligence to be aware of subtleties and undertones, she devotes more than a page to describing society's valuation of him as a graceful dancer, a reliable source of decorating advice, and such safe company for the ladies that not even the most jealous husbands resented his attentions to their wives. He "was neither witty nor handsome; his disposition was retiring; and although he might be seen at any social gathering, he never (except by the excellence of his tailoring) drew attention to himself." Freddy appears not only to have no heroic qualities, but he also seems to lack most of the stereotypical masculine characteristics.

Freddy has a humble opinion of his own abilities as well. He assures his father, "I ain't clever, like Charlie, but I ain't such a sapskull as you think!" But it is Freddy who delivers his clever brother Charlie from the consequences of his own folly; it is Freddy who devises a plan to get Kitty's "smoky" French cousin and the silly young woman whom he loves out of London—and remembers that the lady will need a toothbrush. It is Freddy who remembers a Special License for his cousin Dolph's runaway marriage. Again and again, it is Freddy who demonstrates an aptitude for the kindness and pragmatism that make life saner and more pleasant.

By the novel's end, Kitty has learned to value reality over appearance. She says to Freddy, "I was never in love with Jack in my life…I thought I was, but I know now it was no such thing. He seemed just like all the heroes in books, but I soon found that he is not like them at all." Of course, Freddy is not like the heroes in books either, but by this point Kitty and the reader understand that a truly chivalric nature and a kind heart are to be valued more highly than "all the people one was taught to revere, like Sir Lancelot, and Sir Galahad, and Young Lochinvar, and—and that kind of man!"[16]

Heyer's Mark I and Mark II heroes live on in almost every Regency novel written today. But few will ever compare with the originals.

*~HS~*

**Janga** spent decades teaching literature and writing to groups ranging from twelve-year-olds to college students. She wrote for All About Romance, Heroes and

---

[16] For Heyer's comments on her heroes, I refer readers to Jane Aiken Hodge's *The Private World of Georgette Heyer*. For a fuller discussion, consult Celeste R. Warner's MA thesis: "Heyer's Heroes: An Investigation into Georgette Heyer and Her Literary 'Mark' on the Regency Hero." (University of Waikato, New Zealand, 2010). These scholars informed my discussion.

Heartbreakers, *Romantic Intentions Quarterly* and at her blog Just Janga, where she spent many happy hours immersed in the Regency world.

# 6.

# MY FIRST ROMANCE BOYFRIEND: BEAUVALLET!

## BY DONNA CUMMINGS

When I first started reading romance, most of the heroes were dark, brooding, mysterious and angst-filled men. They were always welcome in my romantic reading fantasies. But there was one hero who stood out from that particular crowd, instigating a lifelong love affair, not only with him, but with others who share his literary DNA.

May I present to you: Sir Nicholas Beauvallet.

He is an English pirate of the Elizabethan era, who falls in love with Dominica, a spirited Spanish noblewoman. He laughs, constantly, especially in the face of danger. He actually courts danger, probably just so he can enjoy another good laugh. The heroine falls in love with him because of his derring-do, but also because he says he will go straight into enemy territory to get her, and he does, cheerfully risking his life, to rescue this woman he loves.

They meet when his crew captures the ship she and her father are on, although the pirates did not know they were aboard. Some of his men hold her captive, until Beauvallet appears on deck:

*Two men went staggering aside, spun apart by an iron hand on the shoulder of each. The lady looked fearfully into the face of El Beauvallet.*

*He had cast aside his morion, and his close black hair showed, curling neatly over his head. Under straight brows she saw fine eyes, the blue of the sea with the sunlight on the water. They were bright eyes and keen, vivid under the black lashes, laughing eyes, watchful yet careless.*

*The laugh was stayed in them now as he checked in his impatient stride. He stood staring; a mobile eyebrow flew*

*up comically; Sir Nicholas Beauvallet appeared
incredulous, and blinked at this unexpected vision.*

*His glance, quick moving, took in next the lady's
captors, and the stilled laughter went right out of his
eyes.*

One of the men gets a fist to the jaw, while the other "was sped
on his way by a shrewd kick to the rearward." Beauvallet apologizes
to Dominica, as though nothing important had happened. And the
heroine's reaction?

*The lady was forced to admit him a personable fellow, and she
found his smile irresistible. She bit back an answering gleam:
one would not smile friendly upon an English freebooter.*

Soon the fiery Dominica has a chance to attack Beauvallet in her
bid to escape, but this is not the kind of romance that is filled with
ravishing and plundering:

*"Good lack!" said Beauvallet, staring down into that
exquisite face of fury. A smile of amusement and of
admiration crept into his eyes. It caused Dona Dominica
to lose the last shreds of her temper. What would you?
She was a maid all fire and spirit. She struck at him, and
he caught her hand and held it, pulled her closer, and
looked down into her face with eyes all a-twinkle.*

*. . .*

*It was not to be borne. The lady's eyes fell, and
encountered the hilt of a dagger in Beauvallet's belt. She
raised them again, held his in a defiant stare, and stole
her hand to the dagger's hilt.*

*Sir Nicholas looked quickly down, saw what she would
be at, and laughed.*

*"Brave lass!" He let her go, let her draw out his
dagger, and flung wide his arms. "Come then! Have at
me!"*

*She stepped back, uncertain and bewildered,
wondering what manner of man was this who could mock
at death itself. "If you touch me I will kill you," she said
through her teeth.*

*Still he came on, twinkling, daring her. She drew back until the bulwarks stayed her.*
*"Now strike!" invited Beauvallet. "I'll swear you have the stomach for it!"*

He turns away, unconcerned, but the heroine is confused, and starts falling head over heels in love with him—just like I did. Ever since, I've been unable to resist irreverent heroes who laugh more than they frown. Who don't take *themselves* too seriously, but are seriously devoted to the strong woman who holds their heart. And who forge ahead even when the obstacles would make a less carefree man call in sick that day.

It's not fair to hold other heroes to the same standard as your first love, because they can pale in comparison. So while the following gents are not intended to be *replicas* of my beloved Beauvallet, they share some traits that bring him to mind:

## 1. Izzy Izzanelli, in Suzanne Brockmann's Navy SEAL Troubleshooter Series

Izzy is actually in several books of the series, but he gets his chance to be the hero in *Breaking the Rules*. Izzy is so irreverent he borders on inappropriate. He sings songs at the top of his lungs, with lyrics that go with whatever situation he finds himself in, even though it would be better if he'd keep his thoughts to himself. He loves hard, falling for a woman who needs his help, and he remains devoted to rescuing her even after she breaks his heart.

## 2. Bobby Tom Denton in *Heaven, Texas* by Susan Elizabeth Phillips

He's a football star, using his good ole boy charm to distract people from how smart and driven he is. He's weary of being fawned over by starstruck female fans who fantasize about being his wife, so he devises a football knowledge test designed to weed out all of them. And when he finds the one who steals his heart, is it any surprise she passes the football test even though she gets most of the answers wrong?

## 3. Davy Dempsey in *Faking It* by Jennifer Crusie

He lies for a living. He's a freelance fraud consultant (aka reformed scam artist). When a character first meets him, she thinks, "He's charming. That can't be good." He uses his quick wit and rakish smile to help the heroine with her quest, even though it conflicts with his own. She keeps him at bay, almost like Dominica did with Beauvallet's dagger, but he still ends up losing his heart, and capturing hers too.

You'd think with such a memorable First Romance Boyfriend as Beauvallet, I'd never have to re-read his story. But I must confess I have re-read his book more than any other, and I have multiple copies of it on my shelf. It always seems to jump right into my cart whenever I am at a bookstore, or online, or a used book sale at the library. I buy yet another copy, as if fearful it will no longer be available to read, and I will have to retell myself the story from memory.

In fact, it's been too long since I've accompanied Beauvallet on his adventures, and it's time to settle back and re-read them again. I highly recommend you do the same.

*~HS~*

**Donna Cummings** has worked as an attorney, winery tasting-room manager, and retail business owner, but nothing beats the thrill of writing humorously-ever-after romances. Her historical titles include *Lord Midnight*, and the four-book Curse of True Love series. She resides in New England, although she fantasizes about spending the rest of her days in a tropical locale, wearing flip flops year-round, or in Regency London, scandalizing the *ton*.

# 7.

## HEYER'S KISSING COUSINS

## BY RUTH WILLIAMSON

In a scene from *Devil's Cub*, Lord Rupert Alastair and his sister-in-law, the Duchess of Avon, have just fetched up at the French inn where their niece Juliana is already staying. She has been travelling with her cousin, the Duchess's wayward son. These lines follow:

> *"Now don't start to make a lot more difficulties!" begged his lordship. "You can't go chasing all over France with a man, and leaving silly letters for a born fool like Elisabeth, and stay single. Why, it's unheard of!"*
> *"I did not go with a – man!" said Juliana, blushing deeply. "I went with my cousin."*
> *"I know you did," said Rupert frankly. "That's what's bothering me."*

In the early chapters of *Regency Buck*, our heroine, Judith Taverner, is living in London with her guardian's cousin, the superbly named Mrs. Scattergood, and has received a visit from her own cousin, Mr. Bernard Taverner.

> *He took her hand, held out to him in farewell, and kissed it. "Dear Judith!" he said.*
> *Mrs Scattergood, coming back into the room at that moment, looked very sharply at him, and made not the smallest attempt to persuade him into staying any longer. He took his leave of both ladies, and bowed himself out.*
> *"You are getting to be excessively intimate with that young gentleman, my love," observed Mrs Scattergood.*
> *"He is my cousin, ma'am," replied Judith tranquilly.*
> *"H'm, yes! I daresay he might be. I have very little notion of cousins, I can tell you. Not that I have anything against Mr. Taverner, my dear. He seems an agreeable creature..."*

In the world of Georgette Heyer, being a cousin does not necessarily confer respectability along with a family connection. It depends upon the cousins concerned. In the hands of this supreme storyteller, cousins run the gamut from staid to stellar, from charming to churlish, from winsome to wicked. By seeing how Heyer employed cousins in a selection of her novels, it will be possible to assess what purpose they serve in her historical fiction.

But first, what is a kissing cousin? While there are conflicting interpretations of the term, in *Brewer's Dictionary of Phrase and Fable* is the following definition: "a relative close enough to be kissed on formal occasions." So, kissing cousins are relations who are recognized as family. In Heyer's Regency world, cousins may be either close or distant. A surprising number of them do end up kissing, and not just as a form of "meet and greet," or as a mere peck on the cheek.

First must come the technical side. First cousins are children of an aunt or of an uncle; second cousins are children of your parents' first cousins; third cousins are children of your parents' second cousins. Your first cousin once removed is the child of your first cousin.

For the purposes of this discussion, Brewer's definition will be adopted, and therefore the kissing cousins in this discussion are those close enough to be kissed.

Before any geneticists begin to feel queasy about marriages between first cousins, we should note that Georgette Heyer was not breaking any laws of the land with her tales of close cousins who marry. It was not illegal for cousins to do so, and for that, we have to thank Henry VIII. Back in 1540, Henry issued a statute that legalized marriage between all first cousins, be they related by blood or through marriage. This remained the case. Later in the 19th century, attitudes changed, especially as genetic inheritance came to be better understood, but in the Georgian and Regency periods, in which Heyer set so many of her novels, there was no legal prohibition against cousin marriage.

Real life Regency and 19th century examples of cousins who married abound, such as the Prince of Wales, later the Regent, who wed his first cousin Princess Caroline of Brunswick in 1795, Charles Darwin, who married his first cousin Emma Wedgwood in 1839, and, closer to the world of literature, Jane Austen's fourth brother Henry married his first cousin Eliza on the last day of 1797. Jane Austen herself created a heroine, Fanny Price, who marries her cousin Edmund at the end of *Mansfield Park*.[17]

To look at Georgette Heyer's own family circle it is best to read Jennifer Kloester's wonderfully comprehensive biography[18] where there are details of Heyer's forebears. She certainly had cousins of her own, and there are some intriguing asides about them in Jane Aiken Hodge's absorbing book, *The Private World of Georgette Heyer*.[19] For instance, Hodge mentions that in the early 1920s it was "...an older cousin [who] remember[ed] Georgette having "such magnetism that when she appeared at a party the young men abandoned everyone else and clustered around her 'like flies round a honey-pot.'" In addition she had older cousins already married while she was still single and writing some of her very early fiction. Much later, during World War II, Heyer not only wrote regularly to one of her husband Ronald's cousins in the Army, but was also named as that cousin's next of kin in case Ronald could not be contacted. Cousins mattered.

So, how did she handle cousinly relationships in her fiction? In September 1922, a magazine published a short story by Heyer, then aged just 20. It was called *A Proposal to Cicely*[20], and its second sentence states that the heroine "glared at her first-cousin once removed." Here Cicely's relationship to her cousin Richard, who is soon recognizable as the hero, shows that these relatives were in her fiction from the beginning. Heyer's characters, even her contemporary ones like Cicely, are part of a world in which people know each other and where their place is, in the family and society.

This is even more so in her Regency novels. There is real evidence that cousins featured in her imagination from the start of her

---

[17] Another example of a suggested cousin marriage occurs when Elizabeth Elliot expects to marry her cousin William Walter Elliot in *Persuasion*.

[18] Jennifer Kloester, *Georgette Heyer: Biography of a Bestseller*, Heinemann, 2011.

[19] Jane Aiken Hodge, *The Private World of Georgette Heyer*, The Bodley Head, 1984.

[20] Mary Fahnestock-Thomas, *Georgette Heyer: A Critical Retrospective*, Prinny World Press, 2001.

writing process. Here is a portion of the advance synopsis she wrote for *The Toll Gate* (1953):

> *Our Hero, little though he knows it, has succeeded to his cousin's earldom, said cousin having had an accident... Another cousin... having discovered where Our Hero is lurking, tries to do him in.*

As it turns out, this plotline is closer to *The Quiet Gentleman* (1951) than to the finished version of *The Toll Gate,* but regardless, this outline contains an integral role for cousins who may even entertain violent intentions towards their kin. We are going to see that kinship, in the form of a cousinly connection, is no bar to ambition or even to murder.

There are very few, if any, of Heyer's historical novels that do not include cousins or at the very least, the mention of them. While what follows is far from being an exhaustive list, the selections used represent some prime examples taken from different stages in Heyer's long writing career.

*The Talisman Ring* was published back in 1936. It contains two sets of heroes and heroines. No less than three out of four of those characters are cousins. First to appear is Sir Tristram Shield, who knows he has no sensibility, is armed with a forbidding expression and might be a hero or a villain. His great uncle Sylvester, the old Lord Lavenham, is upon his deathbed at the start of the action. Tristram, and Sylvester's granddaughter, pretty young Eustacie, are second cousins. It is not long before we learn that young Ludovic Lavenham, disgraced three years before, is Sylvester's grandson and, therefore, Eustacie's first cousin. The old lord had planned for Eustacie to marry Ludovic, but that scheme was scuttled by the disgrace already mentioned.

Another cousin is also at hand. Basil Lavenham is known as the Beau because he adopts the extremes of current male fashion. He is also a great nephew to Sylvester, like Tristram, but unlike him he bears the family name and will inherit all, should something fatal happen to Ludovic.

Understandably the four cousins (Tristram, Eugenie, Basil and Ludovic) regard each other with differing degrees of mistrust and wariness. On occasion both Tristram and the Beau do call Eustacie a "dear cousin," and she also employs "cousin" as a convenient form of address for each of them. When Ludovic comes into the picture, he is not only good looking, but also on the run from the law, an expert shot, and acquires a bullet wound. He is a far more romantic figure than either of his two male cousins. Naturally the attraction between Eustacie and this handsome fugitive is immediate.

In cousin Basil we come to discover something far removed from his dandified exterior. He is revealed to be a villain, no less than a wicked cousin, for in his case, kinship is no guarantee of kindness.

What of the family of the remaining major character, Miss Sarah Thane? She is not related to the Lavenham clan, but her sense of humor, quick wit and appreciation of romance fully qualify her to search for the talisman ring. She also has useful connections of her own, in addition to her brother Hugh, a Justice of the Peace. On several occasions she takes on the mantle of one of her own cousins, no less, to act out the part of a chattering and witless female whose tongue runs away with her. Sarah's cousin is a figure we never actually meet, but her sort is all too familiar.

Ten years later *The Reluctant Widow* (1947) contained another tale of murder and mystery. One Eustace Cheviot is the man our heroine Elinor marries while he is dying. Eustace wants to thwart his autocratic first cousin and former guardian, Lord Carlyon. Carlyon will inherit the rundown estate of Highnoons unless Eustace marries and bequeaths it to his wife. It transpires that the odious Eustace, definitely a loose-screw in Regency parlance, actually suffered his mortal wound at the hands of Carlyon's youngest brother, Nicholas, albeit by accident. Vile Eustace has completely alienated the entire neighborhood, owing to his drinking, gaming and keeping of bad company. Fortunately he expires within hours of his marriage.

Readers are carried along by the pace of events, so they soon accept that not only was young Nicholas innocent of any wrongdoing, but are also comfortable with his rapid adoption of Elinor as a new cousin by marriage. They develop an easy and informal younger brother-older sister style of friendship.

More drama follows, with illicit entry at Highnoons by night, pistol shots, a wound to Nicky's shoulder and a visit by the uncle of the late unlamented Eustace. Just in time for the funeral another relation – a cousin – arrives.

Francis Cheviot is a leader of fashion, a Tulip of the Ton, his appearance is his religion and hypochondria his byword. On arrival, he too asks our heroine if he may call her "cousin." However, outward appearances may be misleading, and there are several twists and turns before we learn just what Francis is really up to.

Elinor has cousins of her own as well, although none she wishes to see. They are "agog with curiosity" about her changed circumstances but she is not keen for their company. Again they are cousins the reader does not actually meet, but their nosy sort is only too familiar. At the conclusion of this tale, our heroine has gained another cousin, for the unflappable Lord Carlyon has declared his hand and heart. He will call Elinor "cousin" in public before she changes her name to his.

During the 1950s Heyer produced no less than ten Regency novels. Of them, it is essential to note the first of that decade, *The Grand Sophy* (1950). Lord Ombersley's large family lives in Berkeley Square and is set on its ears by the arrival of a lively first cousin, who has lived abroad during the time of the Peninsular War. Her sense of style and free manners are daring, yet charming. She is immediately called "Cousin Sophy" by her younger relations, although her eldest cousin, the stern, harsh featured Charles Rivenhall does not admire her and believes she is in need of a set-down. Soon he is moved to say she is "an abominable girl" both to her face and to his straitlaced, humorless fiancée, Miss Eugenia Wraxton.

Sparks begin to fly. Sophy calls Charles her "dear cousin" with a fair degree of irony, but she inspires him to laugh, recognizes his affinity with horses and other animals too. These qualities she can admire, but other traits lead her to describe him as "horrid" upon occasion. By the end of Chapter 6, she has identified what needs to be done for various members of the family, including Charles himself.

Only one chapter later he has unbent enough to call her "Sophy" or even "my dear girl" when he is not annoyed with her, but that state of affairs is short-lived, so that she becomes "cousin" again or even "that wretched girl" when he speaks to his mother about her. Nor is Sophy herself above putting him in his place by reminding her "dear cousin" that he is not the formal master of Ombersley House and that before she came, no one there had dared to flout him. Naturally this puts him into a fury and she is once again his "abominable cousin." When they are not angry with each other, they are just Charles and Sophy and a cousinly relationship is not what preoccupies them. At one stage, she reminds him that she is not one of his sisters and he thanks God for it, but it is clear that both parties actually enjoy their skirmishes. Charles comes to realize that his engagement to Eugenia will mean a lifetime of regret. He cannot cry off with honor, so it will be his abominable cousin who engineers a satisfactory conclusion. These kissing cousins will marry, not because of their family connection, but because they are a match.

*Cotillion* (1953) might be subtitled "a cornucopia of cousins." Its opening chapters introduce four cousins, all great nephews of a capricious but wealthy old skinflint. They have been summoned to his presence so that his heiress apparent, the orphan Kitty, may choose one for her husband. In order to sort out these relationships, a family tree is very useful.

Characters make intricate moves in relationships rather like the cotillion dance itself, and Kitty's first move is to enlist the support of the bemused Honorable Freddy Standen, a noted dancer. Freddy and Kitty are not actually cousins by blood, but all of our heroine's four suitors are first cousins, and they all know each other well.

Different cousins play their parts as the story unfolds, with rakish, charismatic Jack Westruther flirting with his married cousin Meg, and even escorting her to a masked masquerade at the Opera House. Kitty is staying in London with Meg, who has rejected any suggestion that her Cousin Amelia act as her companion. Cousin Amelia is another character who never appears, but who still makes an impact. She remains invisible, but it seems the Standens know just what she is.

This complicated ensemble of some "very dear," a few "ever loving," one "kind" and two or more "not so kind" cousins mingle. Then, Heyer adds still more cousins to the mix. Kitty's beautiful but brainless new friend Olivia Broughty is obliged to reside in London with her vulgar Scorton cousins. Olivia's first cousin, Tom Scorton, is a bore and his sisters are not at all the thing.

Mischief-making Jack brings on to the scene one of Kitty's real relations, none other than her handsome first cousin Camille from France. This is a huge cast, but thanks to Heyer's ingenuity, all cousins fulfil their roles to ensure we reach a neat conclusion, with no less than three happy young couples and one match of rather more mature parties. Four couples are moving in formation when this *Cotillion* ends.[21]

Moving on to the mid-1960s, we have *Frederica* (1965). The bored Marquis of Alverstoke finds himself adopted by the lively Merriville family and addressed as "Cousin" by them, even though his connection to them is very distant. As the Marquis tells our heroine: "I won't even repudiate cousinship" but he implies that he certainly might have done so. By the novel's end Alverstoke is no longer bored, and he will have made the relationship as close as it could possibly be.

Finally in this selection of cousins, we come to *Cousin Kate,* which appeared late in Heyer's writing life. Obviously its title identifies Kate as someone's cousin. Our heroine is certainly Lady Minerva Broome's niece. It follows that Aunt Minerva's son, Torquil, is Kate's cousin. Yet Kate has never met these Broome relations before, and it is because she is an orphan with no financial means of her own that she goes to stay with them, alone and unprotected. Kate's isolation at Staplewood places her in a Gothic setting.

Poor Kate begins to hear things that go bump, and even scream, in the night. Is evil abroad? Her cousin Torquil may be the best looking young man she has ever met, but he grasps her by the throat, and needs a live-in medical minder. Our heroine learns that her aunt is determined that Kate will marry Torquil to provide a future heir, and thus shut out any chance of the estate passing to a Broome nephew, named Philip. When Kate meets Philip, his attitude suggests contempt, and she is quick to deny any kinship. They have no blood connection, but he is soon addressing her as "cousin" for convenience and she does the same. Their personal relationship develops apace.

---

[21] This novel is exactly what one reviewer called it, a prime example of a "Regency Wodehousehold mixup." Refer Mary Fahnestock Thomas, *op cit.*

Later Kate must tell her difficult cousin Torquil why she does not wish to marry him. She explains that it is an "unsuitable alliance." Later she has to spell out what she means to her aunt. Does she dislike the blood cousin connection? In fact, Kate regards marrying Torquil as a mismatch owing to his youth, their lack of love for each other, and her own complete lack of fortune. Such reservations are dismissed by Lady Broome, and events reach a disturbing climax.

In *Cousin Kate,* Heyer has remained within the Regency period, but it feels like we have strayed into a Gothic horror story. Yet this novel, with its uncharacteristic tone, still contains the family relationships, such as those with aunts and cousins, that are a mainstay in Heyer's fiction.

At the end of this survey, what may be concluded about how and why Heyer employed all these cousins? They act as a key adhesive in her novels, like a useful binding agent. They may be many and varied, but these cousins are like mortar.

Mortar is a workable paste and takes many shapes. It binds different materials together, just as the cousin connection links the Standens, Westruthers, Dolphintons and Rattrays in *Cotillion.* It also fills and seals irregular gaps between individual elements, such as we see between Elinor and the Carlyons or between Alverstoke and the Merrivilles in *Frederica.* Sometimes it is almost invisible, like Cousin Amelia Standen, or Sarah Thane's garrulous relation, and at others it adds contrasting colors or patterns to a structure, in the way that Beau Lavenham and Francis Cheviot's styles of dress adorn their scenes like wallpaper.

It is also the mortar that keeps a gap between materials – it divides them – just as loose-screw cousin Eustace Cheviot does, while remaining essential to the whole structure. Often, though, mortar is constructive, so that cousins like the Grand Sophy, and Freddy Standen, act to bring people and families together.

There are many different roles for kissing and other cousins in the world created by Georgette Heyer. To paraphrase W. S. Gilbert, it is by means of "her sisters and her cousins/Whom she reckons up by dozens/And her aunts!" that Heyer's world is made so very rich in background, character, and variety.

*~HS~*

**Ruth Williamson** is forever grateful to the shrewd bookseller who suggested to a bookish young teen that she read *The Talisman Ring*. Ruth is based in New Zealand as an independent writer and commentator, and is currently the editor of the Jane Austen Society of Australia's *Chronicle*. She has taken part in several Georgette Heyer Conferences in Australia, many JASA events, and presented papers to audiences of the Jane Austen Society of North America. She also contributed to *The Joy of Jane,* a collection of essays published to mark 200 years since the death of Jane Austen.

# 8.

# WHAT I OWE TO GEORGETTE HEYER

## BY CHERYL BOLEN

I can't remember the titles of books I've read in the past month, but four decades and many hundreds of books read since, I still remember that *Lady of Quality* was my first Georgette Heyer book. *Lady of Quality* was followed by *The Convenient Marriage*. I was hooked. Little did I know when I discovered Georgette Heyer's books in the 1970s they would have such a dramatic effect on my own life. They were the first historical romance novels I had ever read, and I totally fell in love with them.

How pleased I was to discover this remarkable woman had an impressive catalogue of work. Before the days of internet, it wasn't easy to get my hands on each of her books, but I had a quest. I combed book stores looking for her works. I read all her Regency and Georgian romances, her histories, and her mysteries. I had the pleasure of introducing Georgette Heyer's books to my younger sister, who also devoured each one. Four decades later, I still have every one of those books. Heyer is the only author who has merited her own shelf in my library.

Each book was like a precious journey to another world, a world of men of noble birth and even nobler character, of ladies bound by strictures of a long-gone society, of elegant manners and even more elegant homes that were passed down for generations. I found myself saying things like, "I daresay..." I began to collect fine English porcelain and to crave old silver and crystal. I looked for years for a portrait of a Georgian lady. She now hangs above the mantel in my drawing room.

Even though I was a writer, it never occurred to me I could write the kind of books Heyer wrote. She was The Queen. She had lived in an upper middleclass English family not that many years removed from the period she wrote about—and which she so meticulously researched.

Georgette Heyer is one of a mere handful of authors—J.R.R. Tolkien also comes to mind—who created a genre: the Regency romance. Because of her popularity, many publishers started paperback lines of Regency romances. Once I had read all of Heyer's books, I began to read those other works.

None of them had the essence of a good Heyer book: characters we root for, a reverence for historical accuracy, and her sparkling humor. What those other authors did have was a familiarity with Heyer's works and the Regency world to which she introduced us. They knew Angelo was the fencing master, Jackson instructed gentlemen in the art of pugilism, Tattersall's was where one bought horseflesh, vouchers for Almack's assemblies were eagerly sought, and White's was the gentlemen's club to society's elite. Literally everything we know now about Regency upper-class society came from Heyer.

I judged these other authors against Heyer, and they came up wanting. This is not to say that many of them were not good. Many were very good, especially those who adopted Heyer's practice of adding an "upper class twit" or a similarly inept comedic secondary character.

Before I discovered Heyer, I had imperfectly tried to emulate another great English bestselling writer, Mary Stewart. By day I was a newspaper journalist, by night I wrote mild romantic suspense novels that never got published. In my eagerness to be a published author, I joined writers' organizations and entered contests. I won quite a few, but still no publishing contract.

After judging one of my manuscripts in a contest, the senior editor for Harlequin Historical said she liked my writing and if I ever wrote a book that took place *before* 1900 she would like to see it.

I had never considered writing a historical romance. I was not qualified. I was not a historian. I was no Georgette Heyer. Then I experienced a huge "aha!" moment. Through Georgette Heyer's books I had learned quite a bit about one period of history: Regency England. In fact, I'd gotten to the point where I found errors in books written by Heyer's imitators. Perhaps... perhaps I *could* write a Regency romance.

By then I'd been writing for almost two decades and had been to enough workshops and writers' conferences and read enough books on the craft of writing to have a pretty good idea about starting this new book, my first historical. I wrote the first three chapters and entered them in two contests. I needed to see if this book would fly. It did very well. I finished it and sent it to Harlequin Historical. Several months later an editor called and offered to buy the book, *A Duke Deceived.* It was the seventh full book I'd written but the first historical. A year later, in 1998, it was published to acclaim.

In the twenty years since then, thirty more Regency romances— and a few Best Historical awards—have followed. I owe my rewarding career to Georgette Heyer. I also have her to thank for so many hours of reading pleasure. Rereading a Heyer book every few years is like visiting with cherished friends. Each time I rediscover her genius I am reminded of the awe I felt when reading *Lady of Quality* for the first time.

~HS~

Since being named Notable New Author in 1998, **Cheryl Bolen** has gone on to publish three dozen historical novels set in Georgette Heyer's fictional England. Bolen's books have won many awards and have topped most bestseller lists. In addition, she's been a frequent contributor of non-fiction articles on Georgian England for *The Regency Reader*, *The Quizzing Glass*, and *The Regency Plume* for the past 20 years. Her articles have also appeared in *The Writer* magazine. She lives in Texas.

# 9.

# BATH TANGLE IN THE SOCIAL MEDIA AGE

## BY ANNE-MARIE TURENNE

The title of *Bath Tangle* was remarkably well chosen. This story is nothing but a delightful tangle of misinterpreted sentiments, misguided actions and lots and lots of drama. In quaint, picturesque Bath. Come to think of it, though, it's nothing that we haven't seen in real life. I mean come on, if these people had Facebook...

**Serena Carlow** added a life event: In a Relationship with **Ivo Barrasford**.

**Serena Carlow** changed her relationship status to: It's Complicated.

**Serena Carlow** changed her relationship status to: Single.

**Fanny Spenborough** added a life event: Widowed.

**Serena Carlow** - with **Fanny Spenborough** at **Dower House**: Life is so boring! There is nothing to do around here! #mourning #bored #countrylife #notonparties

**Ivo** said: I told you that you should get a house in Bath!

**Serena** said: And let my cousin ruin my childhood home?

**Ivo** said: There's nothing you can do now, so you should just move to Bath!!

**Serena** said: Selfish!

**Ivo** said: Idiot!

**Emily Laleham** is now friends with **Serena Carlow**, **Fanny Spenborough** and **Ivo Barrasford**.

**Ivo Barrasford** is attending **Quenbury Assembly** with **Emily Laleham** and **27 others**.

**Ivo Barrasford** liked **Emily Laleham**'s profile photo.

**Ivo Barrasford** liked a photo on **Emily Laleham**'s timeline.

**Ivo Barrasford** liked **Emily Laleham**'s post.

**Ivo Barrasford** liked a photo on **Emily Laleham**'s timeline.

**Serena** said: Dude. Ivo, stop liking all of Em's pics! And like some of other girls' too, or else she'll think you're interested.

**Ivo** said: But why, Emily's photos are pretty!

**Serena** said: You don't get it! You can't just like her photos!!

**Ivo Barrasford** - added a photo: with **Emily Laleham** at **Quenbury Assembly**

**Serena** said: Tag the other girl in the pic too!!

**Ivo** said: Who, my niece? Can't remember her name!

**Serena** said: You're so pathetic.

**Serena Carlow** - with **Fanny Spenborough** in **Bath**: Just rented a house for the summer! I love a change of scenery :) #bath #drinkingthewaters #summer #fun #walkingthepumprooms

**Ivo** said: I freaking told you so.

**Serena** said: Shut up!!

**Serena Carlow** is now friends with **Grandma Floore**, **Ned Goring** and **2 others**.

**Hector Kirkby** wrote on **Serena Carlow**'s timeline: SERENA!! IT'S BEEN SO LONG!! TXT MEEEEE (345) 213-4578 :D :D I miss you so much!

**Serena** said: OMG, Hector! I miss you too! Can't wait to talk!! <3

**Hector Kirby** - added a photo - in the **Pump Room** with **Serena Carlow** and **Fanny Spenborough**: #feelingblessed #soinlove #loveyouserena #serenaiadoreyou

**Serena Carlow** added a life event: In a Relationship with **Hector Kirkby**.

**Fanny** said: I'm so happy for you!! Congrats :)

**Hector Kirkby** is now friends with **Fanny Spenborough**.

**Susan Laleham** - at Rotherham House Ball - with **Cordelia Monksleigh**, **Ivo Barrasford**, **Emily Laleham** and **109 others**: This party though! So proud of my daughter, she is the most beautiful girl in the room! - **Ivo Barrasford** likes this.

**Hector Kirby** liked **Fanny Spenborough**'s profile picture.

**Hector** said: You look nice in this photo Fanny.

**Fanny** said: Thank you! Did you see Serena's new photo? She is so beautiful!!

**Hector Kirby** liked **Serena Carlow**'s profile picture.

**Hector** said: My Goddess!! My Queen!! Omg you look so HOT!!

**Ivo** said: Serena you look like a magpie.

**Ivo Barrasford** added a life event: In a Relationship with Emily Laleham.

**Fanny Spenborough** wrote on **Serena Carlow**'s timeline: Serena inbox me, ASAP!!

**Serena** said: What?? What's wrong hun?

**Fanny** said: Did you not see???

**Serena** said: No, what??

**Fanny** said: Ivo!!

**Serena** said: Ivo, what??? He's sick? Ill? Had an accident? Dead?? WHAT HAPPENED?!?!?

**Fanny** said: He's going out with Emily!!

**Serena:** WHAT??? Are you sure?!?

**Susan Laleham** is now friends with **Ivo Barrasford**.

**Susan Laleham** wrote on **Ivo Barrasford**'s timeline: Thank you sooooo much my making my lovely daughter sooooo happyyyy!!!! :D

**Emily Laleham** - feeling **sick**: I can't wait to see you again **Grandma Floore**!

**Fanny Spenborough** liked **Hector Kikby**'s photo.

**Fanny** said: You wanna hang out sometime?

**Hector** said: Sure! Love to :)

**Hector Kirkby** - added a **photo** - with **Fanny Spenborough** in **Bath**.

**Gerard Monksleigh** wrote on **Ivo Barrasford**'s timeline: I EFFIN HATE YOU, YOU RUINED MY LIFE, I NEVER WANT TO TALK TO YOU AGAIN.

**Ivo** said: Hold on, man, da eff is going on?

**Gerard** said: You know what! I hate you!

**Ivo** said: Yeah I got that. But wtf did I do wrong now??

**Gerard** said: Everything!!! Everything is wrong with you!

**Ivo** said: Oh stop being so damn dramatic and just SPIT IT OUT ALREADY!

**Gerard** said: YOU STOLE EMILY FROM ME!!!

**Ivo** said: You love Em? She's in Bath, but don't you DARE go near her!

**Gerard Monksleigh** is now friends with **Emily Laleham**, **Grandma Floore** and **Ned Goring**.

**Emily Laleham** changed her relationship status to: It's Complicated.

**Grandma** said: Em hunny? What's wrong?? Just think how happy you are with Ivo! He is so RICH!

**Emily Laleham** - with **Gerard Monskleigh**: So many hard decisions in life! #feelingpressured #indecisive #needalcohol #somanyproblems

**Fanny Spenborough** wrote on **Serena Carlow**'s timeline: Serena, check your inbox.

**Fanny** said: I don't think Emily is very happy with Ivo.

**Serena** said: Why, what do you mean?

**Fanny** said: Do you not see all her statuses?? I think she's in an abusive relationship!

**Serena** said: What no! Ivo isn't an ogre! He's just very passionate and all...

**Fanny** said: But she's so frightened! I don't think it's healthy for her!

**Serena** said: Ivo clearly loves her, but he probably doesn't show it very well. Emily has no reason to be afraid!

**Hector** said: Fanny, I think Serena and Ivo need to get back together! :P

**Fanny** said: What!! Serena hates Ivo! And besides, she's going out with you!!

**Hector** said: I know... :/

**Gerard Monksleigh** - with **Emily Laleham** going to **Wolverhampton**: Want to travel faster! Can't wait to arrive at destination!

**Serena** said: What are you two doing over there??

**Gerard** said: Nothing, none of your business.

**Serena Carlow** - with **Ned Goring**: Chasing after a pair of crazy children and bringing them back? MISSION ACCOMPLISHED!

**Ivo** said: SERENA!!!! AHKSFJHASKFJH!!! WHAT DA EFF DO YOU THINK YOU'RE DOING?!?!?!

**Serena** said: I'm getting you your girlfriend back, you imbecile! Please don't even think about thanking me!

**Ivo** said: AAARRRGGGGGHHHH!!! I SWEAR!

**Serena** said: Why are you always so bloody mad after me!?! I'm rending you the biggest service I can!

**Ivo** said: I don't want your help!

**Serena** said: I can't effin believe I went to all this trouble to be treated like this!!

**Ivo** said: I DON'T WANT TO BE WITH EMILY!

**Serena** said: WHAT??!? THEN WHY THE HELL DID YOU GO OUT WITH HER IN THE FIRST PLACE?!?!?

**Ivo** said: To make you jealous.

**Serena** said: Don't talk to me EVER again.

**Ivo Barrasford** changed his relationship status to: Single.

**Hector Kirkby** added a life event: In a Relationship with **Fanny Spenborough**.

**Ivo Barrasford** added a life event: Engaged to **Serena Carlow**.

*~HS~*

**Anne-Marie Turenne** has been a Heyerite ever since she first picked up *The Black Moth* when she was eighteen. A whole new world opened up to her then, and she became endlessly fascinated by the Regency era, and the world of historical drama in general. In addition to reading and writing, she enjoys sewing and embroidery, and is currently studying Costume Studies at the undergrad level. She is a tea addict, and loves to collect anything vintage. She lives in Nova Scotia.

# 10.

# FATHERS IN HEYER

# BY JANET WEBB

When it comes to modern fatherhood, these are some likely categories into which our contemporary patriarchs might fall:

- Father Knows Best
- Mr. Mom
- Helicopter Dad
- Hands-off Dad
- Father of Trophy Child(ren)

But what of fathers in Georgette Heyer's historical novels? Where might they fit alongside today's male parental figures?

To answer this question, let us consider the paters in three well-known Heyer tales: Sir Maurice Jettan in *Powder and Patch*; Robert, Viscount Barham in *The Masqueraders*; and Lord Legerwood in *Cotillion*.

I thought initially that the father who had the most in common with our more recent examples would be Freddy's dad, Lord Legerwood. But before long, thinking on it some more, I decided that many of today's fathers are a cross between Viscount Barham and Sir Maurice Jettan.

**Let us start with Sir Maurice.**

*Powder and Patch* was published by Mills & Boon in 1923. Its original title was *The Transformation of Philip Jettan*. Set in the Georgian period, it is full of powdered wigs and patches and poetry – and that's just the men.

According to the back cover (Harlequin edition 2004), young Philip Jettan is too much the country bumpkin to attract Cleone Charteris, the local belle:

> *With his father's encouragement, Philip departs for the courts*
> *of Paris, determined to acquire the social graces and airs of*

*the genteel—and convince Cleone that he is the man most
suited for her hand.*

That's a little misleading, since Sir Maurice and Cleone are hand in glove conspirators, determined to have their handsome, "unpolished cub" shined up into a proper gentleman. There's a definite tinge of Father Knows Best (particularly since Maurice has raised Philip alone after his wife Maria died). Philip is quick to complain to his sophisticated Uncle Tom about his "outrageous sire," like to disinherit his son for his irreproachable and unblemished reputation, but Sir Maurice wants Philip to become a man of the world.

After he is rebuffed by the fair Cleone, Philip does what his father asks and heads to Paris. Months later, Maurice must be thinking, "be careful what you wish for," because Philip returns a changed man.

This being Heyer, most of the changes are on the surface, but both Heyer and Philip enjoy giving Sir Maurice a taste of his own medicine, such as in the letter Philip sends his father, ensconced in the countryside, when he returns to London,

> " ...*as you will observe by the above written address, I have
> returned to this most barbarous land. For how long I shall
> allow myself to be persuaded to remain I cannot tell you, but
> after the affinity of Paris and the charm of the Parisians,
> London is quite unsupportable.*"

**Now, onto Viscount Barham.**

*The Masqueraders* (1928) is set in the time period just after the failed Jacobite Rebellion. I would take issue with the description on the back cover, which says,

> "*Temporarily abandoned by their scapegrace father, Prudence
> and Robin Lacey are forced to masquerade as the opposite sex
> to avoid capture by their political enemies.*"

If scapegrace means careless, that is inaccurate since Prue and Robin's father never stops pulling the strings to control his children's destiny, even though they are often separated because of the exigencies of their circumstances (the fallout after Bonnie Prince Charlie's unsuccessful attempt to become king).

Lord Barham, never shy with self-praise, says to Sir Anthony Fanshawe, Prue's mountainous and perspicacious suitor:

> *"My children are very well. They have beauty and wit—a little.*
> *But in me there is a subtlety such as you don't dream of, sir."*

In the same way that it's satisfying when a Mary Balogh character in her *Slightly* series is able to resolve a difficulty without help from Wulfric, when Lord Barham's children extricate themselves from their double life—with just a little help from Papa—the reader is delighted.

Barham is both self-congratulatory—about his children's achievements, for which he takes almost full credit—and interested in turning the conversation back to that most interesting topic: himself. Barham, in today's parlance, is somewhat of a hovering helicopter father with his two trophy children.

### And finally, Lord Legerwood.

One of the most delightful aspects of reading Georgette Heyer is being introduced to her secondary characters, like the witty and charmingly urbane Lord Legerwood, the amused father of *Cotillion*'s hero, Freddy.

*Cotillion* was published in 1953 and is set at the height of the Regency. Legerwood is a traditional father, leaving the raising of his children to his wife, very much in the aristocratic style. He watches Freddy rise to the occasion of his pretend betrothal to Kitty Charing, in the process turning from an amiable and unprepossessing duckling into a determined and savvy swan.

Don't mistake traditional for hands off though; when Legerwood fears that Freddy needs to marry an heiress, he says to him:

> *"If you've steered your barque of Point Non-Plus, come to me*
> *for a tow, not to a chancy heiress!"*

But loyal Freddy sticks to his guns, and insists that his engagement to Kitty is genuine, leaving Legerwood to tell his wife

Emma that they should do nothing, "Except, perhaps, enjoy a diverting episode."

Freddy's imagination and powers of planning are stretched to the limit by his adventures with Kitty, and no one is more surprised and pleased than his father. When Freddy comes upon the solution of having Kitty stay with his sister Meg, his father takes notice.

> *Lord Legerwood, in the act of raising his claret-glass to his lips, lowered it again, and regarded his son almost with awe. "These unsuspected depths, Frederick — ! I have wronged you!"*
>
> *"Oh, I don't know that, sir!" Freddy said modestly. "I ain't clever, like Charlie, but I ain't such a sapskull as you think!"*
>
> *"I have always known you could not be, my dear boy."*

Of the three, and despite his sardonic quips, Lord Legerwood is the father we'd like to see more of in the world, because he allows his grown-up children the privilege of making their own mistakes and finding their own solutions, thereby gaining for themselves a great deal of wisdom.

But the world is also full of Sir Maurices and Lord Barhams.

What kind of Heyer father is yours?

~HS~

**Janet Webb** is a frequent contributor to All About Romance and *Romantic Intentions Quarterly*. She lives in Canada.

# 11.

# THE GRAND SOPHY: MATCHMAKER OR MASTER MANIPULATOR?

## BY JENNIFER PROFFITT

Nothing says "love" like arriving at your family's house and decreeing they're living their entire lives wrong—and *you* can fix it. Of course, that's *exactly* what the indomitable Sophy thinks upon arrival at her new home with Lord and Lady Ombersley and their children, particularly Charles and Cecilia Rivenhall. Luckily for Sophy, the Rivenhall family is mostly amenable to her appearance in their household—and you have to imagine her cute pet monkey goes a long way towards easing her entry.

As Georgette Heyer has influenced many modern romance novelists, Heyer herself was influenced by Jane Austen—at the very least, the comparisons between *The Grand Sophy* and Austen's *Emma* are undeniable. Much like Emma's machinations with her friend Harriet, which helped Emma see her true feelings for Mr. Knightley, it is Sophy's manipulations on Cecilia's behalf that help her discover her true feelings for her cousin Charles.

Chaos abounds in the Rivenhall household upon our introduction—chaos that stems from Cecilia's love life. While Mr. Augustus Fawnhope is Cecilia's preferred match, he's not the preference of her family, who prefer Lord Charlbury, the "old" mumps-suffering suitor. While Cecilia's mother is sympathetic to Cecilia's affections, Charles has no patience for them. With Lord Ombersley often at his club, and indifferent when home, it is quite clear that Charles runs the Rivenhall household and stands in the way of Cecilia's love for Fawnhope. While Sophy had instantly promised to help Cecilia convince her family that Fawnhope is the one, once Sophy sets eyes on Charlbury for herself at a ball she realizes her earlier pledge to Cecilia cannot be upheld.

Sophy has all the skills and knowledge she'll need to make Charlbury the one Cecilia marries. After all, in order to be the best matchmaker—and really the best manipulator, too—one must know their targets exceedingly well, and living with Cecilia has given Sophy all the information she'll need. It only takes a few meetings with Fawnhope for Sophy to pinpoint the weakness she can manipulate. Fawnhope loves the fantasy of being a poet, and really that's what draws Cecilia to him so much, but neither party has thought of one of the ramifications of their marriage: lack of money. Both Cecilia and Fawnhope have become accustomed to a certain way of life, and while his small allowance can support a bachelor, Fawnhope will need to acquire a profession to support a married life. Knowing this pain point for both sides of this couple, Sophy starts to turn the screws. First, she shares a rather illuminating dance with Fawnhope and lets slip that Cecilia will expect lots of children, saying to Charlbury the next day: "Love in a cottage, you know, and a dozen hopeful children prattling at his knee." While this sentiment doesn't entirely scare off Fawnhope, it starts this couple down a path that's sure to end in heartbreak—or at least, a broken engagement.

Sophy continues to plant her seeds of doubt. When both Charlbury and Fawnhope arrive to visit, Sophy does not discourage Cecilia from the notion that Charlbury has transferred his affections to Sophy. Though, it should be noted that while Sophy uses Cecilia's conflicted feelings to her advantage, she is never cruel about it (unlike the cruelty and thoughtlessness that Sophy's fictional predecessor, Emma, often exhibited), and reassures her cousin that she does not return Charlbury's affection. However, while this jealousy does tip the scale in favor of Charlbury, it is truly his character that helps him win the day. Once Cecilia's sister gets sick, a certain sense of reality—and mortality—sets in for Cecilia. She begins to see the true differences between her two suitors. While Fawnhope offers empty poetry about sick children to ease Cecilia's stress, Charlbury sends flowers from his country estate to the younger Ombersley daughter, simply to cheer her up.

By this point, Cecilia's affections have started to sway from Fawnhope, but Sophy still has one last act of "matchmaking" to execute. As we approach the climax of the book, and the center of Sophy's manipulations, we see her instructing Lord Ombersley to remain firm in his stance against Fawnhope. In a scene that would equate to a Regency "I got this" moment, Sophy steps in to finish the job. So how does she do it? Why, by making Charlbury look "pathetic" enough that Cecilia need not feel guilty for breaking off with poor poet Fawnhope, only to marry a man of fortune and rank. Sophy's solution is to give the appearance she has run off with Charlbury by leaving a rather provocative note for Cecilia to find. This letter leads to a wild chase to track down Sophy before she makes a grave mistake—like ruin herself or marry Charlbury. This chase culminates in one of the funniest scenes of the novel, and has every character joining the hunt before arriving to confront Sophy.

Luckily for Sophy, and unlike Austen's Emma, she suffers from no real ramifications for her actions. Everyone is happily paired off, no one is with someone they shouldn't be, and even Sophy is on the way to having her own happy ending. She has managed to set Cecilia's love life to rights and now it is time to tackle her own. While jealousy helped spur on the affections of Cecilia and Charlbury, they are having a similar effect on Miss Wraxton and Charles. Sophy's behavior has been maddening Charles for much of the novel, but it is when her behavior is juxtaposed against Miss Wraxton's more abrasive traits that Charles finally realizes his feelings for Sophy may be deeper than he first assumed. Even Miss Wraxton acknowledges that she and Charles are ill-suited, having picked up on the underlying emotions between Charles and Sophy, remarking that although she did not love Charles, she was proud enough that she did not want his affections lying elsewhere.

It is ultimately Miss Wraxton's feelings of inferiority, on top of Charles' indifference, that leads to their parting of ways. Sophy's manipulations of the Charlbury situation have delicious consequences for her and Charles, since her efforts on that front unknowingly drive Charles mad with his *own* jealousy. It is this jealousy that ultimately propels their love affair to its final end. After Charles questions Sophy for having the audacity to first be seen about town with the dashing soldier, Sir Vincent, and now to be cavorting with Charlbury, Sophy snaps back, asking what right Charles has to question who she entertains. Of course, dear reader, Sophy is begging Charles to confess his feelings at this point—to profess that his "right" to say anything is that *he* is the only person he wants Sophy seen running around town with. It's one of the novel's few hints that Charles and

Sophy could soon be coming to their own happy ending, as up until then most of Charles and Sophy's scenes are spent bickering.

Early on, it is Lady Ombersley who remarks upon how much Sophy has gotten under Charles' skin:

> *"Good gracious, Charles!... What in the world has she done to put you out?"*
> *He declined to answer this, merely saying that Sophy was pert, headstrong, and so badly brought up that he doubted whether any man would be fool enough to offer for her.*

These are famous last words for Charles, who of course becomes the fool, and so it seems appropriate that in the final line of dialogue they profess their undying love by professing their undying hate:

> *"Charles!" uttered Sophy, shocked. "You cannot love me!"*
> *Mr. Rivenhall pulled the door to behind them, and in a very rough fashion jerked her into his arms, and kissed her. "I don't: I dislike you excessively!" he said savagely.*

Most readers don't leave *The Grand Sophy* thinking they dislike her *excessively*—but they might find they dislike her a little. For the most part, Sophy is incredibly charming and that's what makes her manipulations tolerable, if not even a little altruistic. At the end of the day, Sophy's hilarious lengths to help the ones she loves are a sight to behold, even if you wouldn't want her powers of manipulation turned on your own life.

~HS~

**Jennifer Proffitt** is the former community manager of one of the largest romance community sites, Heroes and Heartbreakers, and now fills her days as a digital marketing professional. She spends her free time writing and reading romance novels and talking about pop culture. She lives in Brooklyn, NY with her cat, whom she likes more than most people.

# 12.

# RELUCTANTLY WATCHING *THE RELUCTANT WIDOW* – HEYER ON FILM

## BY RACHEL HYLAND

Why *The Reluctant Widow*? This must assuredly be the first question any Heyer fan asks when learning that of all her many novels, that is the only one ever to have seen an English language film adaptation. Not that *The Reluctant Widow*, published in 1946, isn't a sprightly take on the Gothic trope (and a far less unsettling one than her later rumination on mental health, *Cousin Kate*). Its heroine, Elinor Rochdale, is a spirited if indigent lady of quality, employed as a governess but soon finding herself embroiled in a flurry of plot featuring deathbed marriages and French spies and suave cousins-in-law. There is great wit to be found in the novel – naturally – and it's all very exciting, all the shenanigans and goings on, along with a very upright, if sometimes infuriatingly bossy, hero in Edward, Lord Carlyon.

But of the Heyer novels available when this film first went into production in 1947, at least a half dozen would have made more sense than the one chosen by its producers. *The Black Moth*, *These Old Shades*, ooh, *The Masqueraders*! *Regency Buck*, *The Corinthian*, *Friday's Child*. All among her best, all full of the requisite story beats and ready-made dialogue that could so easily be translated to the screen. Of course, the simple answer to "Why *The Reluctant Widow*?" is merely that it was the most recent Heyer novel released when financing for a Heyer film at last became available—though the film was not released until four years later, in 1950, for such are the vagaries of the business they call show.

I have to confess that until today I had never seen *The Reluctant Widow* (also known as *The Inheritance*, to US audiences). I have been aware of its existence for at least twenty-five years. Have had ready access to it for at least ten. But knowing that Heyer herself so disliked the adaptation, and hearing nothing but scorn of it from all quarters – the fact that it has vanished without a DVD or legitimate digital trace tells us a lot about its quality – I had made the decision to ignore it entirely, and remain content with the vision of the novel that resides so solidly in my head.

But this morning, in the interests of research, of completeness, and really, just *for you*, dear reader, I essayed the filmic version of *The Reluctant Widow*, and you know what? It's actually... not that bad. At times it's quite excellent, as long as you can think of it as a creation related to, but separate from, the book on which it is based. This is a trick I have learned over recent years, as film and television adaptations of my favorite works are increasingly released, and I am unable to resist seeing them, even though I know they will get it all wrong. I have therefore taught myself to consider them parallel universe versions of the same story, the path-not-taken versions in which there are, variously, added superpowers, conflated characters, missing vital scenes and/or no Tom Bombadil.

The film kicks off with our Elinor unaccountably renamed Helena (Jean Kent), in voiceover, reflecting on how she came to arrive at Highnoons, the ramshackle but enormous estate at which most of the film's hour and a half running time takes place. Kent is beauteous indeed, and carries herself with a true Rochdale regality, employed as a governess by the unseen but already hated Mrs. Macclesfield but mistakenly ending up in the coach of Lord Carlyon (Guy Rolfe), who is attempting to foil his dastardly cousin's plans to marry out of spite. Upon their first acquaintance, the two talk at cross-purposes for what seems like a quarter hour before at last it all becomes clear: she is not who he thinks she is, and he is not who she thinks he is, and certainly, she is not *where* she thinks she is—she took someone else's Uber, and has now crashed a party to which she was not invited.

Helena learns that she has been mistaken for a woman who was to have travelled thither to marry one Eustace Cheviot (Peter Hammond), a wastrel and first-class asshole, who wanted to cut his cousin Carlyon out of inheriting his ramshackle property. But Eustace has been mortally injured in a tussle with the chivalrous Nicky (Anthony Tancred), recently sent down from Oxford and in the wrong place at the wrong time – or the right place at the very right time, if you're the would-be wife whose virtue he was protecting –

and Helena is forced to make a tough decision: either marry Eustace so that he may cut Carlyon out, or allow a posthumous accusation of murder to be levelled at his earnest, quite adorable younger brother.

Of course, Helena goes through with it, because she's a good egg, and also because she really dislikes being a governess, and earning an estate in exchange for a couple of hours unconsummated marriage is a pretty sweet deal. Except! Not only does she now have to deal with the overbearing dictatorship of Lord Carlyon at every turn – telling her what to say and what to do and what she should be worried about and to whom she can speak – but she also has French spies and British traitors and sundry criminal types cluttering up the household at all hours of the day and night. Seriously, people make so free with her house, it's like she's on *Friends*.

Fortunately for my enjoyment of the film, though she is on the brink of leaving multiple times, Helena is a withal courageous and intrepid soul, and moreover is no pushover for Carlyon's particular brand of baron-knows-best bullying. Well... until she is. Things go a little bit haywire in the third act, especially the part where there is a second deathbed wedding – just, *what?* – and also there is an humiliating public inquest into the death of Eustace *which Helena attends*, because sure, plus the arrival of Lord Bridlington (Andrew Cruickshank), Eustace's dissipated uncle, and the debonair Cousin Francis (Julian Dallas) – here renamed Francois, for some reason – who very much attempts to seduce Helena, even though book-Francis is for sure not at all interested in her womanly charms.

Yes, there are some glaring changes from the book to the film, and one enormous oversight: Bouncer, Nicky's faithful canine companion, is nowhere to be seen, it's very sad. There is also a seductive French agent thrown into the mix, one Madame Chevreaux (Kathleen Byron), and even the very premise of the book's beginning – that Lord Carlyon did not wish to inherit Highnoons and all the problems that go with it, and therefore attempted to engineer a marriage in name only between his cousin and a well-compensated wife – is turned on its head, for very little reason at all, and much to the movie's discredit. There is an ingenue, Becky (Lana Morris), brought in as Helena's faithful companion and a flirt for young Nicky, rather than her sensible old governess, Miss "Becky" Beccles; there is another Carlyon brother, John, who is completely absent; and the formal parade ground dishonoring of Lord Carlyon so that he might go undercover as a disgruntled officer eager to turn his coat for the French is made up out of whole cloth. (And is surely an idea taken from a different, much better, film.)

However! If you can ignore the antecedence of this effort, if you can come at it cold – I hadn't read *The Reluctant Widow* in many years before seeing this movie earlier today – then it's a perfectly charming historical romp, with a few nods to Heyer's brand of wit, even if much of the dialogue has been inexplicably rewritten (which: *why?*) and some compelling turns from Jean Kent as Helena, Guy Rolfe as Carlyon and the simply beautiful Justin Dallas – an actor also, and more famously, known as Scott Forbes – as the traitorous Francois Cheviot. Helena gives as good as she gets to Carlyon, to Bridlington, and to Cheviot, and there is one particularly satisfying scene with Madame Chevreaux that almost justifies that lady's existence.

However again! After watching the film I went back and read the novel this afternoon, and there is really no comparison. Those naysayers on the film's worth, when compared with its source material, are entirely correct. But adaptations! Adaptations make books – and authors – famous. A boom in Regency romance – and Janes Austen fever – came about after the hit 1995 BBC adaptation of *Pride and Prejudice*. Agatha Christie reached new fans far and wide after the TV series *Poirot* and *Miss Marple* found dedicated audiences. *Game of Thrones, True Blood, Orange is the New Black, The Handmaid's Tale*. And that's just on the small screen; many hundreds of films based on books have given those books, and their authors, a surge in popularity, in recognition, and in sales as a result of their having been worthy of 3D manifestation.

Why has no successful film or television show yet been made of Georgette Heyer's books, despite many of them having been optioned over the years – most recently, *The Grand Sophy* was once again in development in 2017 – and a built-in audience from among not only Heyer fans, but also the Jane Austen, Masterpiece Theatre and *Downton Abbey* crowd?

It can't be as foolish as one obscure failure, can it? (Two, if you include the 1959 German film *Bezaubernde Arabella*, which you really shouldn't.) I choose to believe it's just that Georgette Heyer is the next filmable frontier. Trollope has been covered. Evelyn Waugh and Forster have had recent series. There's the smash hit that is *Poldark*, of course. And hell, *Outlander*. Surely the wheel of mass media opportunism is bound to come around to Heyer sooner rather than later?

And with any luck, when at last it does happen, and Heyer's particular genius is translated onto screens either big, small or streamed to your favorite device, lessons from *The Reluctant Widow* will be learned. Namely: don't bother with some random parallel universe version of a Heyer novel. These books, these stories, these *words* are perfect, just as they are.

*~HS~*

# 13.

## SPLASH, DASH AND FINESSE! HEYER'S MAGICAL PEN AND INDOMITABLE SPIRIT ON DISPLAY IN *THE MASQUERADERS*

### BY KATHLEEN BALDWIN

Georgette Heyer's heroes and heroines often show sparks of courage, but few have more *savoir-faire* and spunk than Prudence and Robin in *The Masqueraders*. What a challenge Heyer gave herself by attempting to foist on high society a cross-dressing pair of treasonous tricksters, and who are siblings as well. Such an undertaking required its own portion of spunk, and more than a dash of brilliance. This is especially true considering she wrote this entire book while accompanying her mining engineer husband in Tanganyika (now Tanzania), a continent away from her vast personal reference library.

One of the few criticisms leveled at Heyer's work is that she often belabors the period details. However, those critics are viewing her work from our current standards. Heyer's audience in the 1920s would've been far less familiar with Georgian details simply because historical novels had not yet risen to popularity. It fell to Ms. Heyer to educate her readers, and by so doing, she built historical romance readership and a foundation for authors yet to come.

Without Heyer, it is doubtful that the historical romance genre would've taken off as it did. It certainly would've lacked all of the glorious inventiveness it now inspires in writers. As much as I adore Jane Austen, and laud her as the mother of the romantic comedy, without Heyer's out-of-the-box creativity I suspect Austen's charming romance novels would have drifted into the realm of staid historical classics. Instead, Heyer boosted the entire genre into a delightful playground for writers' fertile imaginations, and Georgette Heyer never wrote more out-of-the-box than she did in her 1928 Georgian masterpiece, *The Masqueraders*.

*The Masqueraders* is not for the weak-minded. Indeed, most readers will be slightly befuddled in the opening chapter. Heyer wanted it that way. She does not readily reveal that the two characters we meet in the opening have reversed their gender-roles. She drops subtle hints, but leaves the reader to squint and wonder and then finally, upon making the discovery, say aloud with great satisfaction, "Ahhh! Now I see."

Prudence and her brother Robin have spent their entire lives following after their father, whom they refer to as the Old Gentleman. The old buccaneer has led his children a merry dance throughout Europe and England. Their last adventure landed them on the wrong side of the 1745 Jacobean plot to help Bonnie Prince Charlie regain the throne for the Stuart clan. When that rebellion failed, the Old Gentleman disappeared. Abandoned them entirely. Robin found himself under attainder, which meant he lost the right to any lands or titles he might have inherited, and if captured, he would be hung for treason, or worse, drawn and quartered.

The intrepid brother and sister are not about to let a little thing like a death sentence interfere with their plans. They adopt disguises and march straight into London's Polite Society. Well, not straight. While stopping at an inn on the way, they are called upon to use their clever methods to rescue a young heiress. It seems the lovely young miss has changed her mind about running away to Gretna Green and is now desperate to escape her money-grubbing suitor.

I apologize for that small spoiler and promise not to give away any more plot, except to say that Prudence proves to be a first-rate heroine complete with sword skills, and an astonishing ability to pass herself off as a man. That said, Robin is also miraculously portrayed. Somehow, even though he dresses as a young lady, underneath the face paint the smallish Robin still strikes the reader as masculine. Every time I reread the book I feel like I am studying to try to see how Heyer managed to pull off that magical feat.

Heyer's characters are never dull. Never flat. New writers often ask me about how to write compelling characters. I wish they would all read Heyer and take a lesson from her playbook. Even her secondary characters are engaging. There are only a few two-dimensional characters in any of her books. I think Heyer decided to imbue any character who reappears in her story with some interesting quirk or quality, thus endearing him or her to the reader.

An example of this is Lady Lowestoft's cook, Marthe. Marthe is a secondary character at best, and she only appears sixteen times in the book. Some writers would've glossed over her and given readers a stock figure. Instead, Heyer applies her magic. Not only does Marthe have a distinct dialect sprinkled with French idioms, but she is described so vividly that I want to throw my arms around the woman and give her a hearty hug, just as Robin does when he sees her in London.

Here's Heyer's description of the cook, when we first meet her.

*"The door opened, and the page let in fat Marthe, a tray in her hands. It was a very colossus of a woman, of startling girth, and with a smile that seemed to spread all over the full moon of her face. Like her mistress, from one to the other she looked, and was of a sudden smitten with laughter that shook all her frame like a jelly."*

Notice how, even though Marthe is not a key character, Heyer doesn't scrimp on her description. Her novels are peopled, top to bottom, with rich vivid characters. This is another testament to her stellar creativity.

As we move forward in *The Masqueraders*, we must bow even lower to Georgette Heyer's genius. Here she adroitly weaves an improbable tale of cross-dressing siblings who escape the noose, vanquish evil and bamboozle high society, all while the clever duo falls charmingly and humorously in love with equally interesting counterparts. In *The Masqueraders*, Georgette Heyer convinces us of the impossible. She does so with such finesse and confidence that I firmly believe we are seeing some of the author's own intrepid personality leaking onto the page.

Is it any wonder that after reading *The Masqueraders* I was inspired to take up my pen and write an historical romp? Several historical romps? Heyer inspired me to write heroines who know their way around a dagger and a pistol, young ladies who don't wait around to be rescued, strong female protagonists who splash us with a clever phrase and do it while pushing their captor overboard. Georgette Heyer wrote cool-headed women who possess a healthy dose of gumption and wit, heroines obviously patterned after their maker.

Hats off to you, Madame Heyer! You led the way.

~*HS*~

**Kathleen Baldwin** has written several award-winning Traditional Regency Romances, including *Mistaken Kiss*, a Holt Medallion Finalist, and *Lady Fiasco*. *A School for Unusual Girls,* the first book in her alternate history Stranje House series, was a Junior Library Guild selection, and has received a number of other accolades, while the second book in the series, *Refuge for Masterminds*, won the 2018 GDRWA Booksellers' Best Young Adult award. The series has been optioned by blockbuster producer Ian Bryce, and best-selling author Meg Cabot calls Kathleen's work "completely original and totally engrossing."

# 14.

# HEARING HEYER – HOW AUDIOBOOKS ENHANCE THE EXPERIENCE

## BY KAREN ZACHARY

Georgette Heyer's Regency-era romances are populated with fascinating, sometimes maddening, characters who dress in the style of that day and speak in the manner of that day (no doubt using a good deal more cant than the upper classes actually did). Her meticulous descriptions of manors, townhouses, and carriages easily transport the reader to another place and time.

More than that, however, Heyer is a nonpareil when it comes to dialogue. When her characters speak to one another, it is a joy to read. And if reading them is such a pleasure, imagine how much more gratifying it is to hear those conversations performed by a skilled audiobook narrator. Because I am somewhat of an audiobook addict, I would like to discuss several of my favorites.

### *The Unknown Ajax* (1959)

A major premise of *The Unknown Ajax* is the Darracott family's belief that Hugo, Lord Darracott's previously unknown heir, is an uneducated, uncouth weaver's grandson from the wilds of Yorkshire, when in fact Hugo is a Harrow-educated Army major who is wealthier than anyone else in the family. Hugo learns about the family's disdain for him when he first arrives at Darracott Place and decides to impersonate the bumpkin they believe him to be, primarily by adopting an almost impenetrable Yorkshire accent.

There are moments when Hugo's accent is difficult to read, but in the capable hands of British actor Daniel Philpott, the story comes alive. I'm not familiar with Yorkshire accents, other than watching television programs, but Hugo's voice sounds like the people in *Vera* and the servants in *Downton Abbey*. In other words, Philpott's performance sounds spot on to my uneducated American ear. He manages, somehow, to give the listener a feel for the real, honorable and thoughtful Hugo underneath the ridiculous facade he has adopted.

Like most other Heyer books, the cast of characters is large, but the listener can easily distinguish between the many male voices. Philpott also excels at female voices, and he adeptly handles scenes when many people are in the room talking almost at once.

*The Unknown Ajax* is one of Heyer's funniest Regency romances, and when first reading it, I was struck by what a wonderful play it would make. Listening to this excellent audiobook, however, is the next best thing.

### Frederica (1965)

One of my personal favorite Heyer novels is *Frederica*, the story of the bored, self-centered Marquis of Alverstoke who falls in love with a country spinster, despite the impositions of her younger siblings. Clifford Norgate, another British actor and seasoned audiobook narrator, gives a superior performance. The story does not require that he master many accents, but it does demand that he do something that may indeed be more challenging: sound like young boys, namely twelve-year-old Felix and sixteen-year-old Jessamy. I defy the listener not to be as charmed by scene-stealer Felix as is Alverstoke.

Norgate's Alverstoke voice appropriately captures the world-weariness of the marquis, who is not especially appealing at first, along with his developing tender feelings for Frederica and the two boys. (Sister Charis remains a vexation.) Frederica herself is appropriately calm and mature, if occasionally exasperated by her siblings. Each character's voice is distinct and recognizable, and Norgate also smoothly handles those roomful-of-people-talking-at-once scenes. If Norgate occasionally causes the marquis to sound a bit like Winston Churchill, I can forgive that because of his overall excellent narration of this delightful story.

### Venetia (1958)

*Venetia* must be Heyer's most romantic book, which isn't saying a lot given that her stories are more comedies of manners rather than pure romance. I cannot think of another of her books, however, where the sexual tension compares to this one, so of course hearing Richard

Armitage's mellifluous baritone speaking Damerel's words of love to Venetia may induce swooning. The Armitage version (2010), however, is severely abridged, with about half of the scenes omitted.

Four years later, Naxos Audiobooks commissioned British actress Phyllida Nash to narrate the entire book and her version is first rate. Nash has a deep, honeyed voice, so she has no problems with male voices, and her Damerel is almost as sexy as Armitage's. Unlike some narrators, Nash acts out the part she is speaking, which makes for engaging listening. She is quite good at voicing Venetia and young Aubrey, and her Mrs. Scorrier will make the listener want to throw something.

Nash has performed five other Heyer books: *Arabella*, *Cotillion*, *False Colours*, *The Foundling*, and *The Talisman Ring*. Each one is well worth listening to.

### Black Sheep (1966)

Any Heyer fan should listen to *Black Sheep*, if for nothing more than the hilarious scene where Abigail and Miles meet and she mistakes him for his nephew. This is Heyer at her talkative best. Barbara Leigh-Hunt utterly captures the essence of Miles Calverleigh, this black sheep of his family recently returned from in India. Nothing he does or says gives the impression that he is a wealthy nabob; he dresses casually, ignores the rules of Bath society, and makes his attraction to Abigail apparent long before she is ready to consider a match with him.

Leigh-Hunt is an actress of considerable repute, so I hope to be forgiven when I confess that I sometimes heard Lady Catherine de Bourgh, the role she played so memorably in the 1995 BBC adaptation of *Pride and Prejudice*. Truth to tell, her voice sounds old (she was 74 when this was recorded), and she falls short when voicing thirty-year-old Abigail and her young niece Fanny.

Miles, so different from most Heyer heroes, is the star of this book, so listen to this one for him and for the marvelous banter.

### Bath Tangle (1955)

Another distinguished British actress, Sian Phillips, narrates *Bath Tangle*, the lovers-to-enemies-to-lovers story of Lady Serena and Ivo,

Marquis of Rotherham. Phillips is a very good narrator, particularly when enacting the many heated arguments between Serena and Ivo, perfectly capturing Ivo's aloof, haughty confidence and Serena's fiery, independent self-possession. Indeed it's a pleasure to listen to them bicker. And bicker they do. Since they have known one another all their lives, each one knows how to push the other's buttons.

Phillips does an outstanding job with these two characters; less so with the others, where she does not always differentiate between them sufficiently for the listener to know who is speaking. She is first-rate, though, with one of Heyer's most memorable characters: the fabulously wealthy and happily vulgar Mrs. Floore. (It has occurred to me that Mrs. Floore might match up well with Jonathan Chawleigh, the tender-hearted Cit from *A Civil Contract*).

### *Sylvester* (1957)

British actor Nicholas Rowe narrates *Sylvester, or, the Wicked Uncle* with surprising skill, given that this appears to be his first audiobook. As with *Venetia*, Naxos published an abridged version by Richard Armitage, cutting out more than half of the book. In my opinion, it isn't worth listening to, given that Rowe does just as good a job and in his version the story is not butchered.

Sylvester Rayne is the ultimate handsome top-lofty duke searching for the perfect duchess, and Phoebe Marlowe, small, dowdy, and tongue-tied, is not the one. Their initial meeting is humorous, but also cringe-inducing. As they become better acquainted (yes, snowed in at a country inn), Rowe skillfully adjusts his voicing to better show that Phoebe is in fact witty and intelligent, while Sylvester is kind and genuinely intrigued by the young lady whom he had initially found appalling.

Rowe gives a fine performance enacting the main couple, as well as Sylvester's devoted mother, his drama queen sister-in-law Ianthe, and the absurd tulip of the ton Sir Nugent Fotherby. Moreover, just as Clifford Norgate made Felix the scene-stealer in *Frederica*, Rowe does a wonderful job voicing Sylvester's six-year-old nephew Edmund. Heyer rarely wrote children into her books, but she was skillful at portraying them realistically and with affection.

*Sylvester* was the first Heyer book that I ever read, and I was not especially taken with it. As has happened with some of her others, however, listening to an excellent audio performance helped me better appreciate the book, and it is now among my favorites.

## Heyer's Mysteries

All of Heyer's detective stories are available as audiobooks, and all of them are narrated by Australian actress Ulli Birvé. I have listened to only a few and quite enjoyed them. Customer reviews, however, are all over the map, with the detractors primarily disliking Birvé's languid narration style. On occasion, I have raised by listening speed, but for the most part the pace does not bother me too much given Birvé's excellent vocal characterizations. I have definitely become a fan of Heyer's mysteries in audio format, although her Regencies remain my most-loved.

We Heyer fans are so fortunate that most of her works are now available in audio, and just as we have our preferences with respect to the printed books so also we will be partial to certain audiobooks and narrators. It's just too bad that Richard Armitage can't perform all of them, unabridged, but there is still much pleasure to be derived from hearing Heyer's sparkling dialogue brought to life. If I could recommend only one, it would be the swoon-worthy *Venetia*. Or perhaps the laugh-out-loud funny *Black Sheep*. But then, there's also the charming *Frederica*. Oh, I can't decide, but if you're new to audiobooks, do give one of these wonderful narrations a try.

Hearing Heyer is a whole new experience.

*~HS~*

**Karen Zachary** works as a lawyer in Washington, D.C., a beautiful city largely populated by toad-eaters, elbow crookers, and gabsters peddling bags of moonshine. She revels in reading historical romance, but insists that the history be as authentic as possible. Her book reviews appear online under the *nom de internet* Lady Wesley.

# 15.

# LEARNING! WITH GEORGETTE HEYER

# BY CLARA SHIPMAN

*Nonpareil*. That was what started it, my journal of words I did not know and would have to investigate. I was fourteen years old and just embarking on my Heyer journey, having come across a battered copy of *Frederica* on my grandmother's bookshelf.

"Oh, Heyer," she said, pronouncing it "Hare" in the very proper English way (my grandmother was Cincinnati's answer to a top-lofty dowager duchess). (Top-lofty. That was another word for the journal.) "You will love her. You will never look at those sparkling vampires of yours in the same way again."

She was right.

Ten years later, I look back at my early fumbling with Heyer's beautiful, accomplished language with fond indulgence. Whether it was the slang of the time she wrote so perfectly, the 'pon reps and the Banbury stories and the bits of muslin (maybe a little inappropriate for a teenager), or the elegant use of words that you just don't hear anymore, each Heyer novel was an education in its own right. A glance through my journal shows me I had to look up "florid" and "importuning" and "prodigious," and those are just a few from *The Black Moth*.

And the people! Bonnie Prince Charlie. Golden Ball. William the Conqueror. The Prince Regent. Beau Brummell and Charles Fox and Wellington. Historical figures I'd never heard of and, perhaps, would never have known about, came alive in such a way that studying history became fascinating, essential. I started reading Wikipedia pages about these celebrities of the past *for fun*.

What is most telling is how much good my love of Georgette Heyer's writing has done for my academic achievements. When we studied *Emma* in high school, I found Jane Austen's language a breeze, because I had cut my teeth (another little something for the journal) on Heyer, and did not have to watch *Clueless* to understand what was going on like most of my friends. When we did *Henry V* in

AP English, I had a template for not only the language but also the content, mostly gleaned from *Simon the Coldheart*. When I read *War and Peace* for my freshman Russian Lit class, I understood the context of the Napoleonic Wars and marveled at seeing them from the Russian point of view, having spent so long immersed in them from the English side in *The Spanish Bride* and *An Infamous Army*. I was usually more of a C student, but in those cases I was an A+ brainiac, all thanks to my Heyer-provided education.

But Heyer has helped me more than just in school. Her characters have now burrowed so deeply into my psyche that I consider them as role models—or as cautionary tales. When a boy started a rumor about me in my senior year, even though it added to my consequence (another journal word) I took note from Arabella Tallant's mistakes and immediately denied it to all who would listen. I know what can happen if you let these things run wild, unchecked—and no, it's not that you end up eloping with the much-older nonpareil (that word again) who loves you.

When I started a job right of out of college with a male colleague who thought he could order me around, I channeled my inner Grand Sophy and would not let him intimidate me out of doing what I thought was right. Eventually, he learned to back off and stop micro-managing me. A year later, I became his boss. (And did not end up married to my cousin.)

When a friend and I went on a blind double date but really liked each other's guy, I pulled an Ivo Beresford and made the switch so we wouldn't end up in a Boston Tangle, accidentally dating the wrong people just to be polite. (My friend Lena is now expecting a baby with her guy. You could say that Georgette Heyer created a new human.)

There are those who suggest that the Romance genre is pulpy and unnecessary, that it is derivative and predictable and *bad*. But in Georgette Heyer's work (some of which *is* somewhat derivative, as anyone who has ever read *April Lady* and *The Convenient Marriage* back-to-back can tell you), along with that of many other writers in this field, I have learned more history, more language, and more social graces than from even the most dense and learned history, etymology or self-help books. Not to mention geography! And it doesn't stop there.

It is true than not every lesson in Heyer should be learnt. The elitism of the upper classes, the misogyny and institutional racism, all of that is of its time and definitely not of ours. But even there, seeing what was wrong with the past, feeling echoes of it in our present and constantly striving to do better in our future—there is an easily-absorbed lesson there as well.

Georgette Heyer was a writer with a fanatical attention to historical detail, who included real people in her works and whose vivid word pictures opened up whole new areas of study to a barely-passing fourteen-year-old who was not even motivated enough to read *Wuthering Heights* even though it was Bella Swan's favorite book. It is not an exaggeration to say that reading the novels of Georgette Heyer changed my life.

The cutest part? My grandmother is so proud of herself.

*~HS~*

**Clara Shipman** is a voracious reader of all kinds of Romance, Mystery and Women's Fiction (whatever that is). She lives on the outskirts of Boston, where she spends her days writing algorithms and her nights writing reviews for *Romantic Intentions Quarterly*, when not on long walks with her dog, Lufra.

# 16.

# THE MYSTERY OF *PENHALLOW*

# BY MADELINE PASCHEN

I am not a Georgette Heyer super-fan. In fact, my personal relationship with Heyer and her works would probably be best classified as "casual acquaintances." The truth is that I have only read a handful of Georgette Heyer's fifty-plus books, and only one of her famous romances. (*An Infamous Army*, if you're curious – and yes, it's amazing.) *Penhallow* was the second Georgette Heyer book I ever read, and all I can say is, thank God it wasn't my first. If that was the case, I definitely wouldn't be writing this now, because *Penhallow* would no doubt have been my first and *last* Heyer novel.

*Penhallow,* published in 1942, more than twenty years into her career, is unlike any of Heyer's other mysteries. (It's actually unlike any of Heyer's other novels, period, but we'll get to that.) The story centers around Arthur Penhallow, the patriarch of the titular family. Penhallow rules over his clan – a dysfunctional assortment of adult children, in-laws, second wives, and bastard sons – with an iron fist, using his control of the family finances to bring everyone to heel. It's a classic closed-house murder mystery, and when Penhallow is (spoiler?) found dead, the whole family turns on each other as they try to determine the murderer, bringing ugly secrets and lies to light.

Sounds like a perfectly serviceable mystery setup, if maybe a little too familiar – the "murder at an English country manor" subgenre was all the rage in the 1930s. Heyer had already proven herself to be more than capable of churning out compelling, well-written detective stories, with nine other popular titles in the genre. There's no reason that *Penhallow* shouldn't have been as successful.

Here's the problem, though: *Penhallow* is a terrible mystery. There's no way around it – as a detective novel, it is objectively bad. We, as the reader, start off at an immediate disadvantage when Heyer starts introducing us to the characters (and the potential suspects). Arthur Penhallow, it turns out, has enough children – legitimate and otherwise – to start his own baseball team. In addition to the

Penhallow offspring, a few of them have wives, and Penhallow has a sister *and* a sister-in-law. And of course, the Penhallow family servants have to be included on the list of suspects. So right away, the reader is absolutely *bombarded* with characters, all with their own individual motivations, backstories, and deep dark secrets. The setup to *Penhallow* acts almost like a challenge to the reader, as if Heyer is testing our ability to retain and process all the relevant information.

And it only gets worse from there. Heyer doesn't just set up the family and the circumstances before she hits us with the murder – she takes us along, with painstaking and exacting detail, as each of the extended Penhallow clan goes about his or her day, with each character getting multiple scenes. Reading this book for the first time, I was confused and vaguely worried. *Wasn't this supposed to be a detective story?* I remember thinking. *At what point does this mystery novel involve...you know, a mystery? Am I just going to read about these people being angry and miserable for over four hundred pages?* It definitely felt like Heyer was asleep at the wheel, is what I'm getting at.

And then, when Penhallow finally, *finally* gets the axe (not literally, sadly – he's just poisoned) it happens over halfway through the book! In my copy, which is 457 pages long, the characters find out that Penhallow's dead on page 294. That is a *lot* of setup work. And what's even worse (or even more brazen, depending on your perspective) is that by the time Penhallow is found dead, *the reader already knows who the murderer is*. A few pages before the death, Heyer writes a scene where the murderer – who is identified in the text – sneaks into Penhallow's room and poisons his whiskey. Revealing who the murderer is before the murder even takes place is a bold choice, to say the least. Reading the book for the first time, I wondered if maybe Heyer was trying to be extra clever and mislead us. Maybe, I thought, it'll turn out that Penhallow *didn't* die of poison, and that the whole scene was a giant misdirect! But it's not, and by the end of the book I was left feeling disappointed and frustrated by what an utterly non-mysterious mystery *Penhallow* had been.

That was when I first heard the infamous "contract breaker" rumor. In her 1984 biography, *The Private World of Georgette Heyer* (considered, until recently, to be *the* definitive authority on all things

Heyer), Jane Aiken Hodge writes that Heyer, "vowed to leave [Hodder & Stoughton]. Her contract gave them an option on her next detective story, so she sat down and began *Penhallow*: 'Jimmy the Bastard was polishing the shoes...' Intended as a contract-breaking book, it was duly turned down by Hodder and published by Heinemann."

In other words, Heyer deliberately tanked her own novel to get out of her obligations to a publisher. With that one line, my entire perception of *Penhallow* was changed. Suddenly, what I had viewed as simply a badly-written detective novel became something much more daring. When read as a giant literary middle finger to Heyer's publishers, *Penhallow* becomes almost fun, because you can see how she's going out of her way to write the most boring, plodding, uninteresting murder mystery ever committed to paper. It's not just a bad book, I decided – it's a carefully orchestrated train wreck, and I had to respect how much work it must have taken to tank the novel so thoroughly.

I was all set, as many Heyer fans before me, to accept the myth of the contract breaker. But then came another Heyer biography, this one published in 2011: *Georgette Heyer* by Jennifer Kloester. I read the newer book looking specifically for more information on the *Penhallow* issue, and that was when I learned that everything I thought I knew was wrong.

Not only does Kloester completely reject Hodge's take on *Penhallow,* she has Georgette Heyer's personal letters as proof. The difference is startling: Hodge presented *Penhallow* as a book written out of spite – a deliberate failure created at an extremely low point in the author's life. But Kloester, and Heyer's own letters, show that Heyer was actually very proud of *Penhallow*, and was crushed when critics didn't receive it as warmly as she'd hoped.

According to Kloester's biography, Heyer first got the idea for *Penhallow* when she was working on *Faro's Daughter* – which would be her last Georgian-set novel – and became so obsessed with it that she was unable to concentrate on her current project. She wrote to her agent, L.P. Moore, that the book "will be long, obviously, & more of a problem in psychology than in cold detection. ...this will be a combination murder-story and family saga. It might sweep the board. The family is preposterous enough." She was aware that

Hodder & Stoughton might not like the more scandalous elements she had planned for *Penhallow* – remember, the very first words of the book are "Jimmy the bastard" – but found herself unable to let the idea go. She wrote, "It's no use begging me not to write this book: these astounding people have been maturing in my head for months."

It's easy to see where the idea that *Penhallow* was a deliberate failure originated. Even though she was clearly proud of the book, Heyer knew from the beginning that it would be unlike anything she'd written before. And it's true that due to the publisher's dislike of *Penhallow*, her professional relationship with Hodder & Stoughton fell apart. But the broken contract was an unintended consequence of *Penhallow*, not the goal.

In light of this, I'm kind of amazed that I ever believed the contract breaker story. What author in their right mind would spend so much time and energy writing a book that they *knew* was bad, and that they had no faith in? There have got to be easier ways to get out of a publishing contract besides "write a terrible mystery and risk ruining my reputation as a writer."

So why was I, as were so many others, ready to believe the myth? I think it has to do with the fact that *Penhallow* is indeed unlike anything else Heyer ever wrote. It's not an historical novel, it's *definitely* not a romance, and as detailed above, it's barely a mystery. Dismissing *Penhallow* as a deliberate failure – "no, see, it's bad *on purpose*" – gives us an easy excuse to dislike the book while also allowing us to ignore the possibility that Heyer was experimenting outside her established genres. Maybe that's also why Heyer herself was said to encourage the myth that she'd written *Penhallow* with the intention of dissolving her relationship with her publisher – she was frustrated and upset when the book wasn't well received by critics, and letting the alternate story persist might have soothed her ego a bit.

After I learned all of this, I went back and re-read *Penhallow*. And I realized, to my surprise and delight, that it's actually good. It's a terrible mystery, obviously, but it was never really intended to be one – Heyer even wrote in one of her letters that she "ought to have given it an 18th century setting, and have ruled out the element of detection." *Penhallow* suffers from false advertising more than any lack of quality. And once you approach the book as it was intended –

as the story of a toxic, dysfunctional group of people forced to dredge up all their secrets and grudges in the wake of a tragedy – it becomes a compelling, well-crafted family drama. Despite its vast cast of characters, every single one of them is well-drawn and even charming in their awfulness, and the family dynamics of the dysfunctional Penhallows are almost painfully realistic. It's not laugh-out-loud funny, but the conversations between characters are proof of Heyer's gift for clever, snappy dialogue.

*Penhallow* seems to exist in the Heyer canon much as Jimmy the Bastard does in the story – as the unwanted, unloved reminder of a dark time in its creator's life. But I'd argue that Heyer fans actually owe a lot to *Penhallow* because it's possible that, in its own small way, it helped make Heyer into the author they know and love. After the critical failure of *Penhallow*, Heyer took a break from writing, and didn't publish anything the entire year of 1943 – the first time she'd gone that long without being published in fifteen years. Her next book, published in 1944, was *Friday's Child* – a return to the Regency romances with which she had previously experimented in 1935 (*Regency Buck*) and 1940 (*The Corinthian*), and the beginning of a new era in Heyer's life as a writer.

I'm not going to speculate on how much – or even if – *Penhallow* influenced the creation of *Friday's Child*, or guess what was going on in Heyer's mind during that period between the failure of the former and the bestselling success of the latter. I'm a casual reader, not a Heyer scholar, and those questions are better left to the experts. But I do believe that something crucial happened to Heyer as a writer in that year between the two books. *Penhallow*, regardless of its critical failure, was a passion project for her, and showed her flexing her writing muscles outside of her usual fields.

Whether you love or hate *Penhallow* (and arguments can be made for both interpretations), what cannot be denied is that it represented a crucial turning point in Georgette Heyer's career. It deserves much more recognition and acclaim – certainly more than the "contract breaker" role in which it has been unfairly placed in the popular consciousness.

*~HS~*

101

**Madeline Paschen** graduated from Agnes Scott College with a BA in Creative Writing, with a focus on detective fiction. She lives in Chicago and has written eight novels, one of which she might even publish someday.

# 17.

# BEHIND CLOSED DOORS – SEX IN HEYER'S REGENCY WORLD

## BY ANNA BRADLEY

Georgette Heyer, often mentioned in the same breath as the redoubtable Jane Austen, has been crowned the Queen of Regency Romance by critics and readers alike. We rave about Heyer's command of historical detail, her cleverness and wit, and her understanding of the complexities of 19th century social conventions. She is, and rightly so, the much-beloved font from which all Regency-era romance flows. As author Kate Fenton says in her 2002 article in the *Daily Telegraph*, we've "read her books to ragged shreds."

Heyer's first Regency-era romance, *Regency Buck,* was published in 1935. That was over eighty years ago, which is an eternity in romance novel years. What it is about Heyer's books that still steal our breath? It is the humor, the vibrant characterization, the swoon-worthy romance?

All of the above, but one thing it's definitely not is the sex.

Nor should it be. Heyer, like every writer, was a product of her era. When it comes to sex, the steamier Regency romances of today bear about as much resemblance to Heyer's work as they do to the bodice rippers of the 1970s, where relentlessly alpha heroes with consent issues abound.

Heyer's characters aren't having sex. We might see a kiss and a passionate embrace, but the happily-ever-afters we crave come without a peek behind the bedchamber door. But just because the characters aren't *having* sex doesn't mean Heyer didn't have an opinion about it. She did, and she presents it with remarkable consistency throughout her Regency-era work.

Boys, even in Heyer's decorous world, will be boys. Male sexual promiscuity is treated with surprising frankness in her books. There are multiple references in *Friday's Child* to Lord Sheringham's liaison with an opera dancer. *Cotillion*'s Jack Westruther is scheming to make the beautiful and innocent Olivia Broughty his mistress. Mr. Beaumaris, hero of *Arabella*, is a shameless flirt, and *Frederica*'s Vernon Dauntry, the Marquess of Alverstoke, counts at least one married lady among his string of past lovers. Mistresses, *chéres amie* and "bits o' muslin" are, if vaguely scandalous, treated by Heyer's characters as distasteful, but necessary, evils.

Needless to say, Heyer's heroines don't enjoy the same freedom. This isn't surprising, given the critical importance of a lady's virginity during the era. And it's worth noting that while Heyer's heroines might be admired for their vibrancy, their beauty and their wit, they're rarely *touched* by the hero. We may see a hero grasp a lady's hand to assist her into a carriage. The hero and heroine might waltz together. But physical expressions of affection are usually accompanied by a warning against such risky behavior.

Those characters who do succumb to wild passions and engage in melodramatic displays of amorous excess, such as Charis Merriville and Endymion Dauntry in *Frederica*, or Olivia Broughty and Camille Evron in *Cotillion*, are invariably portrayed as immature, silly, and dull-witted, or even, as in Jack Westruther's case, dangerous. Despite Jack's seductive charm, he's portrayed as selfish, licentious and sordid. Kitty Charing is in love with Jack at the beginning of *Cotillion*, but ultimately, she chooses the sweet-natured Freddy Standen for her husband, and expresses herself vastly relieved not to have been so foolish as to succumb to her initial passion for Jack.

There are a few Heyer heroes who win their heroines despite their inability to control their desires. Perhaps the most notable is George, Lord Wrotham in *Friday's Child*. George, who's got a hint of the Byronesque about him, is arguably the most volatile of Heyer's male creations. He's portrayed as unsteady and too much a slave to his sudden "pets." He's forever flying into rages and challenging his friends to duels, and his approach to courtship is similarly erratic. At one point in the story George forgets himself so entirely as to smother Isabella Milborne in passionate kisses. And though Isabella privately admits she's intrigued by George's excessive ardor, she's also wary of it. George does triumph in the end, but his unpredictability is the reason Isabella initially refuses to take his suit seriously.

More often than not, Heyer's heroes do not give way to their desire for their heroine until they've come to understand that they're in love with them. The reader is left to wonder whether even Sherry and Hero, who are married at the beginning of *Friday's Child*, have consummated their marriage. Early in the book Sherry makes a vague promise not to "trouble" Hero with his attentions, and the reader is made to understand that they keep separate bedchambers. It is only at the end of the book, after Sherry realizes he's in love with Hero, that he ventures to kiss her.

And those kisses thrill us, don't they? Even after eighty years, we still sigh over the kisses Heyer delays until the last pages of her book. Those final moments are particularly delicious, given the previous restraint. In *The Grand Sophy*, Charles, overcome by his passion for Sophy, "…in a very rough fashion jerked her into his arms, and kissed her." Sophy "returned his embrace with fervor, and meekly allowed herself to be led off to the stables." Sophy is one of Heyer's more willful heroines, but immediately after this embrace she's described as "meek." It isn't an adjective that can be applied to her at any other point in the book. One interpretation here is that even the most dynamic heroine will ultimately succumb to a man's more aggressive sexuality.

The sexually passive maiden isn't a popular trope in the current romance market, but this industry has always been particularly nimble in its response to social change. Authors who release multiple books per year are able to react quickly to changes in cultural perspective, and now we're in the midst of a seismic shift in gender attitudes. The romance novels of today reflect that, and with any luck, decades from now readers will be still be sighing over our stories, too.

~*HS*~

**Anna Bradley** is an award-winning author of Regency Romances. Anna came by her love of the era the usual way—via a deep, abiding love for Jane Austen and Georgette Heyer, and an appreciation for gentlemen in breeches and polished Hessians. Anna lives with her husband and two children in Portland, Oregon, where people are delightfully weird and love to read.

# 18.

## READING *THE GREAT ROXHYTHE* – THE LOST HEYER HISTORICAL

## BY RACHEL HYLAND

Even the most ardent of Georgette Heyer fans may be furrowing their brow in confusion right now and wondering what the hell is this book I am proposing to discuss. Did I make it up? Is it some bizarre attempt at Heyer fan fiction? (Which: no. If I was gonna do that, I would totally write a crossover in which Sophia Tallant ends up with Ferdy Fakenham.) Instead, this is one of Heyer's almost legendary Lost Novels, one of six tales that she so despised she refused to allow them to be reprinted within her lifetime.

*The Great Roxhythe* (pronounced "rocks-height") was actually her second published novel, released in 1922. Set from 1668 – 1685, it takes us to the courts of England, France and Holland as its titular counsellor to the king, David, the Most Noble the Marquis of Roxhythe, plays devoted courtier, and secret courier, to Restoration-era Charles II.

Charles II, you see, is in need of some ready cash, and since Parliament refuses to bankroll his excesses, he turns to assorted foreign powers for financial aid. Acting as intermediary in these delicate, secret negotiations is the seemingly indolent Lord Roxhythe, a Royal favorite who will need every ounce of cunning at his disposal to get the job done. (Also, there's religion.)

If you're planning to read *The Great Roxhythe* for the first time, any time, turn away now. Because I am about to break it down for you, in some detail, and apparently spoiler warnings are still required for century-old novels.

If you would, on the other hand, prefer to be saved the trouble, then read on.

Our Lord Roxhythe is a man of exquisite tastes, admired everywhere for his style and panache if not necessarily for his convictions—of which he appears to have none. Strolling through his

King's Court, he is commanded to visit with his royal master, and there he is given a commission: to visit the Prince of Orange at his camp in Holland and ask of him a sum of money in exchange for King Charles's promise to aid his country in their conflict with the French. He meets with two of the King's Councilors to arrange the business, and after working out the strategy for his secret Contiki tour, he asks if either can recommend to him a good man to employ as his secretary. Specifically, he requests one who: "… will be loyal to me; who will transact all the business of the transport for me; who will take orders from no one but me; who will act in implicit obedience to me. In short, gentleman, one who is trustworthy and discreet."

And that is how he comes to meet one Mr. Christopher Dart.

My lord arrives at Dart's home late at night, expecting, it seems, to be instantly recognized. When taxed with his name, he responds with "naïve egotism": "I am Roxhythe." (He's Batman.) Christopher is a very sober young man and seems to have been raised in a virtuous, humorless house – for all the world as though it were on the Prairie – and thus is not immediately won over by my lord's splendor. It does not, however, take long for Roxhythe to cast a spell over young Chris, who takes on the post; it is not very many paragraphs later when "… dislike gave place to amusement and then ripened into liking."

There are, at this time, some excursions and alarums around the King's Court, when it seems the favorite has pissed off the monarch mightily. Of course, Charles loves his "Davy" far too well for this to be true; Christopher, who knows that they are soon to depart for the exotic locale of, er, the Hague in the King's service, suspects that the cold royal shoulder his boss has lately received is merely a "blind for spies." And of course, he is right! Chris doesn't give Roxhythe too much credit for smarts, and so assumes this cunning stratagem must have been someone else's idea (it wasn't), and also believes it "a very brave thing to do." Well, sure. Clearly, he's fearless.

Without any further ceremony, my lord and his secretary set sail for Flushing (known to us by its Dutch name, Vlissingen; but at least now we know how nanny Fran Fine's home got its name), where they meet a Mr. Milward, fellow traveler with an all too apparent interest in Roxhythe and his proposed destination, and who offers his company on the journey. Roxhythe accepts, knowing him to be a spy; he later eludes the interested gaze of other spies by the simple expedient of pretending to be ill and then slipping out the window in the dead of night to go and treat with William of Orange. Sadly, Roxhythe's errand comes to nothing; the Prince, a stern young man of forbidding aspect, is outraged – *outraged!* – by the proposal that he pay tribute to England, and sends my lord away disappointed, in himself and his powers of persuasion as much as in the ruination of his King's plans.

Returning to his sickbed and thence affecting a recovery, Roxhythe and Christopher continue their supposed tour of Holland until the former is called home to Charles's side – his pseudo-slight forgiven – and it is left to him to inform His Majesty that his mission was a failure, because dude just don't play that way. Thwarted, Charles decides instead to seek the money he needs through a different secret alliance: with the French! Let the negotiations begin.

Meanwhile, Christopher Dart, secretary to the stars, is having the time of his life. He is positively smitten with his lord and totally digging his new proximity to greatness. Other people have popped up as major players in Roxhythe's life – Millicent, Lady Crewe, the beautiful teenage newlywed to whom my lord makes elegant advances; Lady Fanny, a cousin and contemporary of the fortyish Marquis, who is perhaps the only person who really understands the complexity that is he. But no one, perhaps not even the King, holds Roxhythe in as much esteem as Chris, who is sure that Roxhythe is the earth and sky, without whom there would be no spring every year, nor would England still be here. (Nor fruit on the tree, a shore by the sea, or crumpets and tea, etc. Chris really likes this guy.) Yet Chris does not see in his idol a terribly clever man, despite their first adventure together, in which Roxhythe bested the cunning minds of assorted Continental agents. Chris thinks of his lord a touch indulgently, believing him to be honorable and decent but unsullied by petty political machinations: none of which, as it turns out, describes Roxhythe at all. Only Lady Fanny – on whom Chris also has a monster-sized crush – suspects the truth of her cousin's influence with, and intrigues on behalf of, the King; the rest of the world thinks him shallow and suave, and trusts him not at all. (One can only assume the young Heyer was a *huge* Baroness Orczy fan.)

They are very right not to trust him; Roxhythe thinks of nothing but his King's pleasure, and sets about solidifying this alliance with the French – in defiance of several existing treaties, as well as the will of Parliament, whom Charles at all times disdains – by the simple expedient of travelling back and forth to France under the pretense of being in love with la Duchesse d'Orléans, King Charles's sister who had been forced to marry King Louis's brother (who is also her cousin). Because being royal is fun! Much is made, throughout the negotiations, of a key point that Charles must accept if he is to become Louis's pensioner: he must re-Catholicify his country, and outlaw Protestantism, which by this stage had been the national religion of England for over a century (yeah, thanks for all the wars, Henry VIII!). His brother James is all for this, since he's a Catholic from way back – to the point where he gets a little... er... energetic when at war with the Protestants up north; yeah, thanks for all the wars, Henry VIII! – but Charles comes out with a really cool law, the Royal Declaration of Indulgence, which allows everyone to follow whatever religion they want to without fear of reprisals or beheading.

It turns out to be a weirdly unpopular law, and gets almost instantly repealed; apparently people liked all the beheadings. Man, they needed Netflix.

Back in the not-on-Charles-II's-Wikipedia-page portion of the narrative, Lady Crewe's husband, Sir Henry, is getting crosser and crosser at the three-year long flirtation in which his wife has indulged with Roxhythe. She had been hopelessly devoted to her husband when a new bride, but has grown distant and cold as her fascination with the unscrupulous Marquis heated up. He is but playing, but she is in earnest, and before long Sir Henry just can't take it anymore. He challenges Roxhythe to a duel (denied), then challenges him again (denied) and then finally just goes ahead and shoots him in the chest, because a man can only take so much, and probably also because it took so long to load those old timey pistols that it would have seemed a waste of time not to go ahead and use it once you had. Happily, it's only a flesh wound (suck it, Sir Henry), but the Crewes must perforce immediately leave the country following an attack on the King's favorite, and Roxhythe, who was supposed to leave the country himself to deliver yet more messages to Louis re: Charles's pocket money, now cannot.

So he sends the devoted Christopher instead. It is the beginning of the end.

Christopher's very dour brother, Roderick, we met earlier when he disapprovingly allowed Roxhythe to visit with William of Orange that one time. Roderick, in company with almost every other character in the book save the King and Roxhythe himself, has repeatedly begged Chris to leave the service of his lord, whom he considers all kinds of dodgy; it is this trip to Holland that finally does it, however, when Chris – surprisingly not as oblivious as he has heretofore seemed – discovers that he was used as a conduit to make a non-sanctioned deal with the hated France, selling his beloved country to the highest bidder. Roxhythe had not wanted to use Chris in this way, for he had discovered in his selfish heart that "In some vague way, Christopher's presence was necessary to his happiness." But in the end, the needs of his King outweighed his own need for an adoring secretary who would kiss his hand and lavish him with praise 24/7. And thus: schism, and one far more dramatic in the context of this story than the divide between Catholic and Protestant.

After nine years of faithful service, Chris leaves Roxhythe, jaded, bitter, disillusioned, heartbroken. He goes to work for various politicos, but none give him job satisfaction so eventually he ends up in the service of his brother's man crush, William of Orange. The Prince is all set to marry King Charles's niece, the Lady Mary, and all kinds of riots and rumpuses are occurring throughout the land – Catholics are being put to death, conspirators against the King are being put to death, good men who have political enemies are being put to death, there is so much death because history is really just all about death. Also, Charles's eldest son – illegitimate, as are all his children – is part of a plot to overthrow the Crown. Roxhythe turns double agent and pretends to be a part of the cabal, eventually bringing about their downfall. Hurrah! Charles is safe! Except, no, he gets sick and dies, because this was the 17th century and one could be King and still basically die of a hangnail.

Roxhythe is sad. And now pretty much everyone fears and/or hates him. James takes the throne, and wants to throw his brother's favorite in the Tower. The conspirators that favorite betrayed are worried he knows too much, and might foil Monmouth's rebellion, version 2.0. Christopher is still in Holland, and sends word to Lady Fanny to pass on his sympathies to his "deare Master", and that he is "looking forward eagerly to the Day when I may once againe press His Hand" – but that day will never come (sorry, Chris), because all too soon Roxhythe takes a bullet to the chest in a drive-by – no, more a walk-by – shooting that he made no effort to stop. In fact, it was kind of a Suicide by Cop situation; without his King, his lordly life is simply not worth living, and so he allows himself to be gunned down like a bewigged gangsta rapper, later saying from his deathbed: "Dear Fanny—all my difficulties are solved."

Then, reminiscences… delirium… death.

*Finis.*

Huh.

So *that's* why Heyer didn't like it.

In the Foreword to the 1977 posthumous paperback edition of *Simon the Coldheart* (another of her suppressed works), Heyer's son said that his mother was "her own sternest critic" and that "in this instance at all events, her judgment had been too harsh." As *Simon the Coldheart* is one of my Top 10 favorite Heyer novels ever, I could not agree with this verdict more; in the case of *The Great Roxhythe* however, I am totally on his Mum's side. Because… damn.

Look, it's not like this book doesn't have its virtues. For one, Roxhythe himself is the very model of the witty, quippy, laconic anti-hero with which Heyer first began experimenting in *The Black Moth*. Tracy Belmanoir, Duke of Andover, is the spiritual ancestor of David, the Marquis of Roxhythe just as Vernon, Marquis of Alverstoke and his excellent secretary Mr. Trevor (cf. *Frederica*) are the spiritual heirs of Roxhythe and Christopher Dart. However, just as Tracy was made too villainous to ever be redeemed, and thus was made over into the less objectionable Justin, Duke of Avon in *These Old Shades*, Roxhythe is rather too coldblooded, too unlikeable to be a true hero for us here. For example, even after he has been ill-used by his lord shamefully, Chris comes to him seeking his help for an acquaintance of theirs who was to be executed for a crime he did not commit.

> *"My dear Chris!"* expostulated Roxhythe. *"Do you expect me to meddle in these low matters?"*

Chris wants him to ask the King to intervene, but Roxhythe won't even consider it:

> *"The King is not omnipotent, Chris. The public will not be content unless some blood is shed. If he interferes they will turn on him. His position is precarious."*

Roxhythe is so in love with his King that the concepts of right and justice elude him. In fact, Roxhythe himself had recommended innocent men be put to death, because it was the will of the people and would make Charles's life easier:

> *"I thought you knew that nothing counts with me save His Majesty's safety and peace?"*

Yeah, nice guy.

That "His Majesty's" there, though — that is clearly a typo. Because the evidence given elsewhere throughout the book suggests that it should have been rendered as "His Majesty his peace," which I at first found quite grating in its execution but by the end of the novel found utterly charming. Georgette Heyer is always making me wonder at this language that is ours, and here as nowhere else she does so by the simple expedient of removing apostrophes. Look at the title of Chapter II: "The King His Councillors"; Today, it would be "the King's Councillors", of course, and sound far less romantic and ye olde as a result. So throughout the novel it's "The King his this" and "the Prince his that," which of course is because back in the days of which she writes, the accepted possessive abbreviation had yet to become common practice... except, how does one then explain Shakespeare? (Seriously, I'm asking. Any Shakespearean scholars in the house who can riddle me that?)

Speaking of scholars, Heyer's dab hand at the history stuff is certainly on display here, and is impressive as hell, except that it's also a little... well...dry. It's almost like this novel started out as a high school essay on the power struggle between the Catholics and the Protestants in Stuart-era England, or even of the political machinations undertaken by Charles II, or even of Charles II and his many mistresses (some of whom he made duchesses in their own right, just for sleeping with him – nice work if you can get it?). There are opaque references to personalities and laws and parliamentary procedures, and the reader is given perhaps a shade too much credit for personal knowledge of some fairly obscure historical events. Perhaps one day Showtime will air a series called *The Stuarts*, and we'll come to know all there is to know about such things – or, at least, all there is to know that is vaguely accurate and portrayed by people with far too sparkling teeth for the era – but until then, this book had me awash in a sea of bubbling confusion for pretty much the duration.

The most notable thing about this book, however... and especially, in a Georgette Heyer novel? Hardly any romance at all. Of bromance, there is much – Roxhythe and Charles; Chris and Roxhythe; Chris's boring brother and William of Orange; assorted nobles and the Duke of Monmouth, pretender to the throne, etc. – but aside from Roxhythe's unkind dalliance with the immature Lady Crewe, and passing reference to others of that nature, there is really nothing here. All the emotion is reserved for the guys, and boy, are they not afraid to show it. Let us go back to that earlier passage, in which Roxhythe confessed his perfidy to Chris:

> *"Oh—oh, heaven, how I wish I had never laid eyes on you!"*
> *Roxhythe stretched out his hand.*
> *"Chris, dear boy, you are demented. Calm yourself."*
> *Christopher ignored his hand.*
> *"Then 'tis you have driven me so! You did your best to break my heart—and now you reveal yourself to me— callous! Ruthless! It—hurts damnably, my lord."*

Even after this, Roxhythe begs Chris to return to him, but to no avail, for Chris won't "sacrifice my honor for love of man." No wonder he never gets himself a girlfriend—not that we even meet with any prospects for such. Lady Fanny's pretty cool, and Chris adores her, but she's married; in fact, all the protestations of affection in this book are either between married people to others who are not their spouses or between liege lord and humble servant. It's... weird.

Even before reading *The Great Roxhythe* (available digitally and also bound with elegant simplicity from boutique publisher Amereon House – my 2006 edition was part of a print run of only 200 copies, or so it claims), I had found Heyer's dense historical works to be of limited interest. Oh, I always loved *The Spanish Bride* – based on a true story of love amid the Napoleonic wars; you just kind of have to ignore the fact that our heroine is fourteen – and had a soft spot for *The Conqueror* – can you guess who that one's about? – but *Royal Escape* and her unfinished master work, *My Lord John,* I found dense and difficult and depressing. Alone of Heyer's other historical novels, I have only read them once.

As for *The Great Roxhythe*... as a Heyer completist, I am glad to have had the experience of it. Also, there is much of her nascent genius to be enjoyed in these pages, in particular her way with a natty Frenchman – seen here in the person of Roxhythe's friend, M. le Comte de Saint-Aignan – and her talent for a lazy, sardonic rejoinder. Also, I shed genuine tears when I reached the not-at-all shocking end; there was just something so poetic about a supreme egoist like Roxhythe – I mean, he even refers to himself in the third person!; wow, he really *is* like a gangsta rapper – basically going into a decline for want of his BFF.

But man am I glad that it wasn't readily available back when I first started reading Georgette Heyer novels, because had this been my introduction to her work, I don't know that I'd have carried on. I mean, the author herself wanted all mention of this book stricken from the record, and yet allowed *Cousin Kate* to remain on library shelves everywhere.

That says it all, really.

*~HS~*

# 19.

## BEAUX, BELLES AND BLACK SHEEP – THE FACTS AMONG THE FICTION IN THE BATH BOOKS OF GEORGETTE HEYER

### BY KIRSTEN ELLIOTT

Bath is a city that prides itself on its literary connections, from Geoffrey Chaucer and his saucy Wife of Bath to Peter Lovesey's irascible 21st century detective, Superintendent Diamond. However, many of the writers of whom the city is so proud hated the place. They often agreed with Horace Walpole, who said:

> *I dislike the place exceedingly, and am disappointed in it.*
> *Their new buildings that are so admired, look like a collection*
> *of little hospitals; the rest is detestable; and all crammed*
> *together, and surrounded with perpendicular hills that have no*
> *beauty.* [22]

He decided to return home, although he was not cured, declaring:

> *They may say what they will, but it does one ten times more*
> *good to leave Bath than to go to it.*

Jane Austen's opinion on finally leaving Bath was little different from Walpole's. Writing to her sister Cassandra in 1808 she recalled that:

> *It will be two years to-morrow since we left Bath for Clifton,*
> *with what happy feelings of escape!*

Bizarrely, Jane Austen is now celebrated in the very city she disliked by an annual festival. Yet her opinion was positively benign compared with that of Dickens. Both of his Bath books, *Pickwick Papers* and *Bleak House*, present a very jaundiced view of the city. It was in decline at the time, but Dickens's descriptions are particularly

---

[22] Letter to the Honorable H.S. Conway, October 1766.

cruel. On one visit he called it "a mouldy old roosting place." In 1867, he wrote to a friend, Mrs. Dickinson:

*Don't come to Bath. I hate the people and only read there at Chappell's[23] solicitations.*

Despite this, he was also the subject of celebrations in the city in the early 20th century. The city has not fared much better at the hands of modern writers. Although John Betjeman loved the Georgian architecture, he deplored later alterations such as the removal of glazing bars in the windows. Above all, he hated what was happening to the city in the 1960s, during what became known as the Sack of Bath. His poem *The Newest Bath Guide* concludes:

*Now houses are 'units' and people are digits,*
*And Bath has been planned into quarters for midgets.*
*Official designs are aggressively neuter,*
*The Puritan work of an eyeless computer.*

*Goodbye to old Bath! We who loved you are sorry*
*They're carting you off by developer's lorry.*

When Dr. Andrew Swift and I wrote our book *Literary Walks in Bath*, we looked at the city from the viewpoint of such writers, but our book was unusual in that it also included a walk based on the Bath books of Georgette Heyer[24]. Despite having written more books which include Bath than any of the writers mentioned above except Peter Lovesey, she is the one author about whom Bath keeps silent. If a visitor mentions her name to some Bath guides or local historians they will be subjected to, at best, a pitying sigh or, at worst, a patronizing sneer.

The reason for this remains a mystery. Her books are well-written and carefully crafted. She was a close friend of the biographer Carola Oman, and shared her love of history. She has fans worldwide, among them the Booker Prize-winner A. S. Byatt, feminist Germaine Greer and Queen Elizabeth II. Yet it was only in

---

[23] Samuel Arthur Chappell (1834-1904), youngest son of Samuel Chappell, of Chappell & Co., music publishers, who promoted and organized Dickens's Penny Readings.
[24] I have used some excerpts from the walk in the text of this essay.

2015 that English Heritage decided to honor her Wimbledon home with a blue plaque. At least this is a step forward, unlike in Bath, where she is ignored. When I created a walk for the 2002 Bath Literature Festival, which I called "Beaux, Belles and Black Sheep – Georgette Heyer's Bath," I promoted it by saying the walk was:

> *A chance for fans of Georgette Heyer to come out of the closet and hold their heads high! Sometimes today derided for her romantic novels, in fact Miss Heyer carried out exhaustive research before writing each book. Kirsten Elliott looks at the city she described and discusses how accurate a picture of Regency Bath her novels provided.*

It is a sad reflection on the lack of esteem in which she is held that I felt impelled to advertise it in that way – so credit goes to Bath Festivals for allowing me to do so.

If anyone is new to Georgette Heyer's Regency novels, they could not do better than read the five books in which Bath features. Not only do they give indications of the writers who influenced her, they also tell us something of how her writing style was affected by her own circumstances. They were written over a period of 30 years, and just as the youthful exuberance of Austen's *Northanger Abbey* is noticeably missing from the more somber *Persuasion*, so the joyful romp of the first, *Friday's Child,* with its childlike heroine who is starry-eyed about her often thoughtless suitor, is a far cry from the dysfunctional families portrayed in her last book, *Lady of Quality*, with its mature heroine. Written when Heyer had already been suffering ill-health for a time, it was to be her last novel. She died of lung cancer in 1974, two years after its publication.

Between these two come *The Foundling* (1948), *Bath Tangle* (1955) – perhaps the least satisfactory, as it was written in a hurry and under financial pressure – and *Black Sheep*, published in 1966. However, for me, it was her historic research which proved particularly interesting and I became engrossed in tracking down her primary sources. Fortunately I owned some, and had used library and archive versions of others.

One of her principal sources on Bath was the *Improved Bath Guide*, also known as the *Original Bath Guide*. Unfortunately, it was not always reliable. In my various fields of research, I had already discovered that, just as today's publications are not always accurate, the same faults occurred in the past. Heyer assumed – wrongly – that if people were writing at the time they ought to know what they were talking about. *The Guide* is particularly culpable. It came out almost every year, but was frequently a reprint of earlier editions and changes were not always picked up. This led Heyer into an uncharacteristic mistake over one of the real characters who finds his way into the novels. None of the tales is set earlier than 1816, but throughout them all, she refers to the Master of Ceremonies at the Lower Assembly Rooms as Mr. Guynette, as do the *Guides*. However, he had smartly absconded some time in 1815. Although passing himself off as a Frenchman, he came from Guernsey, and was married with a family in Bath. All seemed to be going well, but the Rooms, despite redecorations, were struggling, and the lessee, Finegan, blamed his financial woes on Guynette[25]. The Master of Ceremonies was arrested for debt, but jumped bail and hurriedly left for London. Thanks to an advertisement offering £10 for his arrest, we know what he looked like:

*About 40 years of age, 5 feet 6 inches high, black hair with large mustachios, long black whiskers with dark complexion, is generally dressed in blue Cossack pantaloons, black coat with a blue regimental long great coat, braided in front; has a genteel appearance and address, walks very spright and quick.*

As late as 1818, the *Original Bath Guide* still gave the impression that Guynette held the post of Master of Ceremonies at the Lower Rooms. He died, aged 70, in 1843. Life had not been kind to him – he set up as a builder, but was again declared bankrupt in 1830. Perhaps it is better to imagine him, as Heyer did, reigning over the rooms and being charming to the ladies.

Another trap for the unwary is the *Guide*'s map. It often shows developments that were intended but never built, as Bath slid out of fashion into genteel respectability, and the country endured a series of financial crises caused by the Napoleonic Wars. In most cases, Heyer was careful to include sites which can still be enjoyed today, but in two of the books she has people walking and even living in

---

[25] Also spelt Guyenette.

Lower Camden Place or strolling in the gardens there. These are certainly shown on the map, but the houses were never built nor the gardens laid out. The ground was unstable, and Camden Crescent itself – known then as Camden Place – was left incomplete due to a landslip. By and large, however, Heyer is accurate. She certainly does not make the blunder made by Dickens in *Pickwick Papers*, when he succeeded in confusing the Royal Crescent with the Circus.

Nevertheless, the *Guides* were invaluable sources for Heyer, giving background color to her scenes set in Bath. The rules for the Assembly Rooms, to which she frequently refers, come from their pages, including the fact that the Upper and Lower Rooms had different hours. She correctly places Mr. King as Master of Ceremonies at the Upper Rooms. Other little snippets often caught her eye. She seems to have been intrigued by the Harmonic Society, about which the guides wax lyrical. This society was really as much about drinking, dining and conviviality as singing. Despite some of the clubs attracting serious composers, the standard of singing after five hours must have left much to be desired. Heyer was aware of this – its efforts are castigated by one of her characters as "infernal howling," a comment which may have been inspired by a contemporary description of an event at a domestic glee club, where the tenor singer wrote:

> *How we got to the end I scarcely know: but of all the execrable music that was ever howled by any Infernals, the discord, yell and grumbling... could never be exceeded.* [26]

The *Guides* also contain details of many charities. It was doubtless here that Heyer noticed the Stranger's Friend Society, based in New King Street, which makes a fleeting appearance in *Lady of Quality*. Founded by the Methodists in 1790, it was run from the Wesleyan chapel, and was non-judgmental. All the applicant had to prove was that they were in distress, and aid was provided, regardless of its causes.

Perhaps one of the most interesting real-life characters mentioned in the novels is Dr. Wilkinson. Wilkinson was a surgeon from London who first appeared in Bath in 1803. By 1804, he was

---

[26] From *Recollections of the Life of Richard John Samuel Stevens*, 1793.

offering a course of three lectures in Galvanism at the Lower Rooms. By this time he was becoming established as one of the country's leading exponents of Galvanism. By 1807, he was entitled to call himself Dr Wilkinson[27]. His lectures continued, first at Hetling House, near the Hot and Cross Baths, and then, in 1809, at Kingston House, where he set up a lecture room and his own laboratory. In December 1809 he advertised in the *Bath Chronicle* that he had taken over the privately-owned Kingston Baths, and had enlarged and improved them, adding a vapor bath.

He – or rather his baths – make an appearance in *Friday's Child* and *Black Sheep*, while the doctor himself also advises on the health of one of the characters in the latter book.

As well as contemporary local newspapers, which Heyer may well have consulted, it is probable she used the postal directories that were beginning to appear fairly regularly at this time. In particular, she would have found *Gye's Bath directory, corrected to Jan. 1819* a mine of information, giving details of local interest such as where to hire servants and where to find day schools for girls.

Also published in 1819 was Pierce Egan's *Walks through Bath*. There are clear indications that she had read – and possibly owned – a copy. Egan was an expert on boxing and Heyer must have come across his book *Boxiana, or, Sketches of Ancient and Modern Pugilism*, when she was researching this subject, about which she knew a great deal. In the book of walks she would have found a very full description of Sydney Gardens. It was Jane Austen's favorite part of Bath so we should not be surprised that the gardens appear in three of Heyer's books.

What is intriguing is how she knew so much about Bath's best-known inns. She doubtless acquired the names of many from the directories, while in his opening chapter of *Walks in Bath*, Pierce Egan described the York House as:

> ... *a fine building, and considered one of the largest and best inns in the kingdom, out of London. Its accommodations are in the first style of excellence, under the superintendence of*

---

[27] In an advertisement in the *Bath Chronicle* (5 March 1807), Wilkinson describes himself as "of the Philosophical Societies of Manchester and Newcastle and Associate of the Institute of Medicine of Paris."

*Messrs. Lucas and Reilly. In the season it overflows with company of the highest rank in life. The dining-room is equal, if not superior, to the large room at the Crown and Anchor, in London. The suite of rooms correspond, and are furnished in the most superb manner... Stages also set out from the York-House every day for London.*

So we can see why she chose it for the wealthy, and people of high status. She knew, too, that The Pelican was no longer in the top rank of inns but still respectable. Perhaps she got her hands on J. F. Meehan's little pamphlet *A Few Famous Inns of Bath & District*. But Meehan says almost nothing about the Christopher Inn, so how did she find out that it was famed for its respectability? It had been run by Methodists since 1745, the then-landlord being an acquaintance of John Wesley, the religion's co-founder. It was so respectable that in 1782 the landlord would not subscribe towards the prizes for the Bath Races, the only landlord in Bath to refuse[28]. Thus *Lady of Quality*'s overly-respectable Lady Elmore stays there, while more rackety characters have lodgings in the lively White Hart, an inn so noisy that Jane Austen's friend Fanny Cage found it intolerable and moved to quieter Bathwick[29].

Georgette Heyer would also have discovered much about inns, especially those in the countryside around Bath, from *Paterson's Roads*. Daniel Paterson was an army officer, and his first Road Book listed the mileages of military marches. However, by 1776 he was publishing regular versions of what he called a *"Delineation and Description of the Roads of Great Britain."* These were small books that could be handily slipped into a greatcoat pocket and supplied the reader with routes and mileages of most coach roads, along with brief descriptions of sights along the way. Paterson was appointed Lieutenant Governor of Quebec in 1812, and ceased producing them, so in 1822 a London publisher called Edward Mogg, believing that Daniel Paterson was dead, brought out a new version. This was far more extensive and was certainly not pocket-sized. However, the detail is incredible, differentiating between towns and cities, noting which had markets, and which inns supplied post-horses. This

---

[28] *Bath Journal*, 16 September 1782.
[29] Letter to Cassandra Austen, 15 September 1813.

information was irresistible to Heyer, and it features in many of her novels. Most notably, the route in *Bath Tangle* that Serena Carlow and Ned Goring take to pursue an eloping young couple can be traced directly from this book, as well as the route taken by the fleeing youngsters.

Certainly, Heyer also absorbed much information from other fiction writers, including Robert Louis Stevenson. In *The Foundling*, there is an amusing but ruthless villain whose character is very like that of Long John Silver. There can be little doubt that this is deliberate, for his name is Liversedge, the first six characters of which are an anagram of Silver.

Heyer's books are full of these subtle in-jokes, none more so than *Black Sheep,* which has many sly references to one of her favorite authors, Jane Austen. Even the heroine, Abigail Wendover, bears a striking resemblance to Jane herself, even to living in Sydney Place.

This essay just touches on some aspects of Georgette Heyer's research. Others have written about her exhaustive studies of fashionable costume, which was ground-breaking at the time. Very few people considered costume worthy of serious historical study; indeed, it was regarded as rather trivial. Now the study is widely respected and you find exhibitions in museums worldwide, including the Victoria & Albert in London, and the Fashion Museum in Bath.

So is it time for the academic world to reassess the value of Heyer's books as it has the subject of costume research? Hilary Mantel's historical novel *Wolf Hall* received glowing reviews. The *New York Times* described it as dazzling. Yet it is still fiction— though, like Heyer's novels, it was the product of hours of careful study. Why, then, is Georgette Heyer's work in historical fiction regarded as somehow unworthy of serious consideration?

It is my hope that this essay shows some of the lengths to which she was prepared to go to ensure accuracy in her novels, and that Bath's local historians, guides and literary critics will begin to give her the respect she deserves.

*~HS~*

**Kirsten Elliott** has always had an interest in industrial archaeology, particularly canals, but her other interests are architecture, dance, literature and the social life of the Georgian period. For over thirty years she has led guided tours of Bath, and she also professionally researches the history of buildings. She is the author of several books on Bath's literary, architectural and social history.

# 20.

# RETURNING TO HEYER – HOW I CAME TO APPRECIATE THE SLOW BURN

## BY MEGAN OSMOND

When I was four years old, my parents divorced and my siblings and I went to live with our father in a small country town, several hours away from my mother. The custody arrangement saw my siblings and I make the trip to stay with our mother during school holidays. With great foresight, she maintained contact with the girl who had been my best friend prior to leaving, and the holidays became an opportunity not only to see my mother, but to be reunited with Rachel. To see which one of us had grown taller over the school term, obsess over Olivia Newton-John, play with My Little Ponies and Barbie dolls, and so on. Of course, such childish pursuits were eventually outgrown – with the exception of Our Livvy – and on the cusp of becoming teenagers, Rachel and I turned our attention to romance novels.

This is where our tastes began to part ways. We both delved into Barbara Cartland, but where Rachel gleefully accessed her mother's vast library of Georgette Heyer novels, I was unable to see the appeal in such chaste narratives, and preferred writers such as Marion Chesney and, later, Stephanie Laurens, where the romance was front and center, and occasionally torrid if I were lucky. Rachel continued to implore me to read Heyer and I did read one, but the plot was too slow for me, the romance too implied rather than explicit, and there was barely a kiss, let alone a sex scene. Nope. Bodice-rippers were my thing, and Rachel could keep her quaint Georgette Heyers to herself.

I know when things changed and I began to love Heyer, but I don't know why. Probably age, experience, and patience. Whereas I had found the romance too slow and too far in the background as a teenager, I now understood the depth of emotion that could sit behind a glance, and the constraints of the time, which are generally wildly over-looked in the bodice-rippers. I had postnatal depression with both of my children, which would trigger anxiety attacks when I breastfed. I found that distracting myself with something light-hearted was the key to reducing stress, and my memories of breastfeeding my son are now interwoven with watching and re-watching *Sex and the City*, *Frasier*, *The Big Bang Theory*, and *The Office*.

Of course, once I had my daughter a couple of years later, the TV would be more often tuned into children's shows, and so I purchased a Kindle – which I had then so far resisted, being old-school about *real* books – and began to read. What I began to read, for reasons I can't recall, was the entire catalogue of Georgette Heyer, and I loved every one of them. I began with the more accessible romances: the clever Venetia and her irresistible anti-hero, Damerel; the delightfully activist Arabella and the debonair Robert, who is always one step ahead; Miss Trent frustrating the progression of her romance, through self-exclusion and misunderstanding, with the emotionally-intelligent Waldo in *The Nonesuch*; the masterful and haughty Ravenscar brought to his knees despite himself in *Faro's Daughter*, and so on.

Having exhausted the most appealing titles, I moved onto the less appealing ones. I didn't really *want* to read about romance between first cousins, but nevertheless hugely enjoyed *The Grand Sophy*. 18th century men's apparel doesn't do it for me, but Avon's red heels didn't detract from *These Old Shades*. A shy young hero? I wouldn't have thought it, having always preferred slightly cynical, worldly-wise alpha types, yet *The Foundling* was another win. In fact, although I naturally have my favorites, there wasn't a Georgette Heyer novel I didn't enjoy, even if I didn't like the premise. That speaks to the genius of her prose – the bullseye characterizations and scene-setting, the clever dialogue, the subtle slow burn romance, all of it seemingly effortless. Of course, there are some aspects of her work that don't sit so well in a modern context, but I don't generally subscribe to the view that we should throw away great work because the artist, or a theme or characterization within the work itself, is problematic. Heyer wrote in her time, we read in ours, and so it goes.

My daughter is now long past the age of breastfeeding, but rereading Heyer will always remind me of rocking gently and quietly in my chair, my baby girl asleep in my arms, holding my Kindle and burning through novel after novel. I'm glad she was so prolific. I'm even gladder that I had the good fortune to have a friend who turned me on to her work, even if there was a twenty-year delay between recommendation and uptake. Lastly, I'm glad we had mothers who held the candle of our friendship until the flame was strong enough to burn on its own.

*~HS~*

**Megan Osmond** uses her Ph.D. in molecular biology to read the chemistry between characters in romance novels. She is a frequent contributor to *Romantic Intentions Quarterly*. She lives north of Sydney, with her husband and two children.

# 21.

# THE LOST CONTEMPORARIES – A SLIPPERY SLOPE

## BY MAURA TAN

When the editor of this essay collection, the... er... *persuasive* Rachel Hyland, approached me about joining in on the fun of Georgette Heyer commentary, I just stared at her, confused. She knows how I feel about historical novels, whether romantic or otherwise: which is to say, not very much. So, what could I possibly contribute to this discussion of the world's greatest historical romance novelist? (I may not read it, but I know the biggest names in the field I don't read.)

But then Rachel handed me four hardbound volumes in a deep maroon: *Instead of the Thorn, Helen, Pastel*, and *Barren Corn*. And then she said, simply: "Read these."

Because Georgette Heyer, it turns out, also wrote contemporary fiction. And that is very much in my wheelhouse.

It is unsurprising that even I, an aspiring reader of all the contemporary fiction the world has ever produced, was previously unaware that Heyer had dabbled in my favorite genre. It is well-known among the Heyer faithful that she was not pleased with these four books, and suppressed their republication (along with two historical novels, *The Great Roxhythe* and *Simon the Coldheart*) throughout her lifetime. They were first released from 1923 to 1930, after which she never wrote a straight contemporary novel again, all the way until her death in 1975. For an author to be so scared away from a genre for forty-five years, after several attempts across almost a decade to get it right, shows that there was clearly something lacking in these novels, or perhaps in the reception they received. I was eager to delve into them, and see quite what it was that had Rachel – the self-described "Heyerest Heyer fan who ever Heyered" – so keen to get my take.

I began with Heyer's first contemporary, *Instead of the Thorn*, and understood right away. Rachel figured I would *love* these books. She knows I have a fondness for social commentary, and raw emotion, and awkward, obviously autobiographical, detail, and *Instead of the Thorn* has all of that in spades.

*Instead of the Thorn* is the sorry tale of young Elizabeth Arden – I know! – who is raised in London of the 1920s as though it was London of the 1890s. Her aunt is a forbidding, Victorian-era tyrant, and Elizabeth is raised in a seen-and-not-heard, meek-and-shrinking, girls-know-nothing kind of way. At nineteen, Elizabeth meets the dashing, well-bred Stephen, a writer, and he finds he simply *must* marry her, because she is so pretty and innocent and he can't bear to think of anyone else, well, owning her. (*Mine! Mine!* thinks Stephen. Gross.) But Elizabeth knows literally nothing about how the world works, how people work, and most definitely not about how marriage works, and so she spends the next hundred or so pages being just a big wet sap who you would definitely want to send along to some kind of therapist, if she were a friend of yours, or at least give a copy of *Everywoman* to. She's like Carrie, but without the pyrokinetic homicidal tendencies. She is so ignorant of basic life necessities that you, too, will want to dump pig's blood on her more than once. And as for Stephen! Threatening to rape your virgin bride because she won't put out… not on, man. Not on.

I've checked, and Heyer was not married when this book was written – it was published when she was only twenty-one, in 1923, and she wed George Ronald Rougier in 1925. So this was not, as I had hoped, a thinly veiled account of her own marital teething problems – I do love literature that acts as schadenfreude – but it does feel like there is a lot here that might well be taken from her own experience. Particularly, Elizabeth's aversion to being touched by her husband (with whom she is legitimately infatuated, though it would be hard to call what Elizabeth feels anything as mature as love) reads, in a modern context, like asexuality—or somewhere else on the LGBTQI+ spectrum. That is always a fun possibility to speculate about, in the lives of these writers from past, much more reserved, eras. Of course, it could also denote something much darker, and not at all fun to speculate about. All I know is, if taken in a certain light, *Instead of the Thorn* reads kind of like a cry for help.

Or perhaps the unmarried Heyer was simply working through her fears of adulthood with this novel; or she was exploring her own insecurities about her place in the modern world; or perhaps she had a friend or relative who was going through a truly horrible time with an abusive asshole (and Stephen, though not the worst offender among Heyer's contemporary "heroes," is definitely abusive, as well as being controlling in the extreme). Or, as has been frequently suggested, maybe she was just *young*, and wanted to write a book that might gain her serious notice from critics and scholars, in the vein of something that might be penned by an Evelyn Waugh or an E. M. Forster. Certainly, her famously comedic style and witty dialogue is absent here, though there can be no denying that Heyer knew how to build a character and turn a phrase.

*Helen*, Heyer's next contemporary effort, is even less funny, except that it is funny how it is so very uncomfortable to read. (But I like that sort of thing.) Here we have another weak-willed heroine, and one with a giant-sized father complex it is hard to ignore. The story begins with said heroine – Helen, obviously – as a child, and we see her grow up into a hopeful writer who fortunately has a family fortune to fall back on, since she never quite manages to be as productive as she hopes. When World War I breaks out, almost every man Helen knows signs up for "the adventure" and we are given a chilling, tragic portrait of literally toxic masculinity. Meanwhile Helen spends the book outraged by a) feminism, b) socialism, c) activism, d) bohemianism, e) divorce and f) any man not her father.

Heyer's biographers, Joan Aiken Hodge[30] and Jennifer Kloester[31], both report that this novel was her most "autobiographical," and it is a very revealing self-portrait, if that is so. But also, could this not have been Heyer being ironic? The unlikeable Helen surely could not have been how she saw herself, could it? I am choosing to believe not. I want to believe that Helen is a caricature of a prudish, snobbish, conservative reactionary with an Oedipal complex, and not a reflection of an actual person that existed

---

[30] Hodge, Joan Aiken, *The Private World of Georgette Heyer*, The Bodley Head, 1984.
[31] Kloester, Jennifer, *Georgette Heyer: Biography of a Bestseller*, William Heinemann, 2011.

at one time, and whose work people worship. And if taken in that light, *Helen* is a work of genius indeed.

Even if it is not, it's still well worth the read, just for how painfully exposing it probably is.

Much lighter in tone is the next contemporary in her book list, *Pastel*. In many ways, this is kind of *Sense and Sensibility* fan fiction, except with a much bleaker outlook. Like Austen's classic, it deals with two very different sisters, one of them always exasperated by the other one. But here, elder sister Frances is overshadowed by the lovely younger Evelyn and, instead of being indulgent and understanding and a good example to us all, in proper Elinor style, she flounces about the place feeling ill-used and competitive, but in a competition she can never win. It's actually very realistic. (I should note, here, that I have sisters.)

The autobiographical element, we are told by experts, is the girls' distant mother, and I can totally understand why Heyer would have wanted to retract this apparently thinly-veiled slight against the woman gave birth to her and was still alive to know about that slight. (I should note, here, that I have a mother.) But *Pastel* is also a psychological treatise as much as it is a childhood catharsis, and it's by far the funniest of the contemporaries – there is even a dog! *Pastel* is a book in the mode of, say, Elinor Glyn or Anthony Trollope. It even has shades of P. G. Wodehouse about it, in its more laugh out loud moments, which alone of the contemporaries, it does have. It is a fascinating look into the time, into family expectations, and into one shy, but sly, woman's envious head. It's a book about what lies beneath the surface, and is certainly the most enjoyable of the four contemporaries – even if, again, you want to slap its whiny heroine across the face a bunch of times.

To me, the least enjoyable of the four is 1930's *Barren Corn*, and good golly, I don't even understand how this was written by the same person who penned *Pastel*, let alone by someone renowned for her lively romantic fiction. This one is all about class, and pretty much no one in it has any. Here we meet the irretrievably awful Hugh, an aristocratic idiot who decides to marry lovely shop girl Laura on a whim (that whim being that she won't sleep with him until he does) and then inherits a barony and discovers that she is ALL WRONG for his social station. Laura is swept off her feet by the attentions of this posh suitor, but as she struggles with the minutia of a world for which she wasn't raised – it's like that part in *Pretty Woman* where Vivian doesn't know how to use the snail tongs, but *all the time* – and Hugh refuses to give her the least bit of help or try to find anything they might have in common, or maybe just find a way to not be such a major dick, she wishes she were back in her shop, and so do we.

Classism exists in the world to this day, of course, and it was even more of a thing in the London of the 1920s in which this tale is set. Laura is pretty affluent by today's standards – her family even has a servant – but they dare to work for their living in menial ways, and are actually kind to each other, unlike the gossipy, backstabby brutality of Hugh's friends and family. I have seen *Barren Corn* described as a book that illustrated its author's prejudices against the lower classes, but I am not sure I agree. Everyone in this book who is from the so-called upper classes is just trash. Laura's family are great. And true, Laura is another of Heyer's contemporary heroines who needs to be stabbed in the eye with her own hatpin (which she barely knows how to use), but much of that is the fault of Hugh, and the general aura of feudal superiority that surrounds him and his cronies, as much as it is her own weakness.

So, I didn't enjoy *Barren Corn*. But then, neither did I particularly enjoy *Middlemarch*, or *Tess of the D'Urbervilles*, or *Lady Chatterly's Lover*, but all are classics that are read and reread and studied and examined, because of what they say about the times in which they were written, and about the frailties of the human condition, and about the humans who wrote them. And of the Heyer contemporaries, and for all its flaws, *Barren Corn* belongs in the same breath as those works of undeniable genius, because as grueling a read as it truly is, what it has to say about dynastic wealth, social class, ethics, kindness, cruelty and compatibility is absolutely worth reading. You just probably won't want to read it again.

So, the question becomes: what does Heyer have to offer the reader of contemporary fiction? I would say that she has a lot. It is easy to see why she'd have preferred to hide these books – someone so notoriously private would doubtless not relish having so much of her inner thoughts put on display for all the world to see. But that is a big part of what makes them so fascinating. As I said, I like fiction that acts as schadenfreude, and there is a lot here that is exquisitely uncomfortable; if an acquaintance were to tell you half this stuff about themselves, you would consider it too much information. But also, these books have a lot to say about their time – the gusto with which all those men signed up for World War I in *Helen* will forever haunt me – and they give one a lot to consider about changing attitudes and social mores. Even when you're furious about the misogyny you're also pleased at how very far we've come in such a relatively short time.

"Like when Bertie Wooster dresses up in blackface," said our editor, when I returned these books to her and was forced to admit how glad I was to have read them.

She'd stared at me expectantly, until I shrugged my shoulders in defeat and sighed. "I loved them."

"I knew it!" she exclaimed, grinning wide, and then reached into her bag, bringing out a stack of old, well-worn paperbacks.

"Now, did I ever mention Georgette Heyer also wrote contemporary crime novels?"

I guess I read Heyer now. I'll probably be reading Regency Romance before the year is out. And I am strangely fine with it. It's a slippery slope, isn't it?

*~HS~*

**Maura Tan** was born in Zanzibar, grew up in Morocco and lives in Singapore, where she is currently studying for her third degree in Contemporary Literature—when not writing reviews for *Romantic Intentions Quarterly* and eating her bodyweight in durian.

# 22.

# GAMBLING IN HEYER
# BY RACHEL HYLAND

Whist. *Vingt et un.* Hazard and Loo and Faro and Piquet. If you have ever read an historical romance, and certainly one set in London between, say, the two Queens Elizabeth, then chances are you have come across reference to at least a few, if not all, of these games of chance, once popular with the ruling elite. Only *Vingt et un* remains with us virtually unchanged – you might know it as Blackjack – though both Whist and Hazard have survived in modified form, as Bridge and Craps respectively. But even the most enthusiastic of today's high rollers would be hard put to call themselves as dedicated to Lady Luck as were the scions of the Upper Ten Thousand back in the days of yore, for whom gambling was as much occupation as it was hobby and/or addiction. It was like they were an entire class of World Championship Poker players, only with less tattoos (though, possibly the same number of wigs).

Historical Romance would have us believe that every second gentleman of breeding spent much of his time at the gambling table – or gaming table, as it was much more pleasingly known; "gaming" has a much nerdier connotation now, of course – winning and losing enormous sums, bonding in the camaraderie of excess, and becoming accidentally, often resentfully, engaged to some benighted fellow's innocent young daughter, sister or (soon-to-be) widow.

I must confess that I harbor a not-so-secret love of Barbara Cartland's Heyer-imitating, historical nonsense, dating back to my adolescent adoration of her enduringly adolescent works featuring doe-eyed, heart-faced virgins with mostly made up names: Zenobia, Aldora, Salrina, et al. Often the recycled plots of these foolish fancies would feature a Forced to Marry motif in which a rakish young man would wager his broken down ancestral home against some equally broken down gamester's worldly goods, and when the inevitable happened and the Not Our Hero lost, his subsequent suicide would leave Actually Our Hero with no honorable option but to marry his late opponent's doe-eyed, heart-faced virgin of a daughter. Switch out the rakish, penurious young man for a sardonic, thirty-something nonpareil who comes to survey his newly-won country house only to find it inhabited by his late opponent's doe-eyed, heart-faced virgin of a sister, and you have another variation on the theme. Other books and plots brought gambling into the action in other ways – *A Hazard of Hearts* had our hero's mother an addict and probable cheat; *An Angel in Hell* had our heroine playing roulette in Monte Carlo with our hero's also-addict mother; etc. very etc. – but the prevalence of storyline-propelling financial ruin due to a love of cards, dice and horse racing in the Cartlandian oeuvre certainly gave the impression that such a calamity happened all the damn time.

And she wasn't far off. Oh, it's doubtful that quite as many (say it with me) doe-eyed, heart-faced virgins found the domineering loves of their lives due to their suicided guardian's predilections and compulsions, as her – and many others' – fiction might suggest. But the reality is, enormous gambling debts caused fashion icon Beau Brummell to flee England and otherwise capable statesman Charles Fox to lose much political power. The Duke of Wellington, that battlefield nemesis of Napoleon himself, almost had to leave the Army as a lieutenant to pay his gaming debts. And some couples really were Forced to Marry, with the likes of the Earl of March being wed at eighteen to a thirteen-year-old girl in payment for his father the Duke of Richmond's bad luck.

In her book on the eponymous 17th century beauty – and gambler – *Georgiana: Duchess of Devonshire* (filmed as *The Duchess*, starring Keira Knightley), Amanda Foreman states: "Gaming was to the aristocracy what gin was to the lower classes: it caused the ruin families and corrupted people's lives." She goes on to quote noted contemporary wit Horace Walpole: "A thousand meadows and cornfields are staked at every throw, and as many villages lost as in the earthquake that overwhelmed Herculaneum and Pompeii." It was a time when anything as uncouth as gainful employment was considered beyond the pale for the well-bred, and when the lucky sperm Masters of the Universe had at their disposal the livelihoods of their whole families, as well as their tenants and servants, such was their dynastic wealth. At least three months of the year – the Season – were to be spent in the metropolis engaging in an orgy of ever-increasing frivolity, away from even the smallest demands of estate and household management. Throw in marital disharmony the likes of that experienced by our poor Georgiana, and it is really no wonder that even for those who did not develop a full-blown obsession, gaming added excitement and a feeling of satisfaction to an otherwise dull, perhaps even unproductive, life. As Georgette Heyer's young Hubert Rivenhall tells his stern elder brother Charles, a trifle defiantly, in *The Grand Sophy*: "I wish I had not had such infamous luck, but everyone plays, after all!"

There is a reason that in her very first novel, the Georgian tour de force that is 1921's *The Black Moth*, Georgette Heyer put gaming very much at the fore, with our hero exiled from Polite Society due to an accusation of cheating at cards. (Dude don't play that way, of course. He'd not be our hero, else!) Gaming was so prevalent in the upper class echelon in which Heyer laid her scene that including at least some mention of it, in its various permutations, was an entirely essential element in lending veracity to her past milieu.

Other of her novels feature newly-fledged young misses fleeced of kisses, jewels and pin money in assorted games of chance (*Powder and Patch*, *The Convenient Marriage*, *April Lady*), young blades befriended and cheated by smooth-talking "Captain Sharps" (*Arabella*, *Frederica*, *Friday's Child*) and family fortunes brought to the brink by ruinous play (*The Grand Sophy*, *Venetia*, *A Civil Contract*). The much beloved *These Old Shades* feels like it takes place almost exclusively in Parisian gambling establishments – the Duke of Avon repaired his fortunes by winning someone else's, let's recall – and *Faro's Daughter* assuredly does, with our heroine actually a hostess of same. (!) Indeed, there is not a single one of Heyer's thirty-two historical romances that does not mention some form of gambling, whether it be a simple game of lottery tickets among the schoolroom set or a serious I-might-blow-my-brains-out-if-I-lose turn of a card in a tense gentlemen's club showdown.

More recent historical novels, both Trad and blush-inducing, keep this tradition begun by Heyer very much alive, with the likes of Lisa Kleypas's *Dreaming of You* (part of her series The Gamblers) having a hero who runs a gaming hell – a "hell" being the equivalent of a modern-day backroom high stakes poker game – and Julianne McLean's *The Prince's Bride* (part of her Royal Trilogy) featuring a heroine who kidnaps a man – fortuitously, her One True Love – in order to pay her father's gambling debts. House parties, card parties and visits to exclusive gentlemen's clubs like White's and Brooks's (which yet exist) still abound across the various subgenres, and if I had a dollar for every beta character who found himself with pockets to let after a particularly disastrous visit to Ascot or Tattersalls, I'd doubtless have enough to pay off all of their cumulative losses— probably even with the couple of centuries worth of interest.

Of course, gambling remains an incredibly popular pastime to this day – with global casino revenue alone estimated at over $115 billion in 2016 – and while it is definitely a more egalitarian endeavor now, it was hardly the preserve of only the *ton* even back in Heyer's chosen time periods. Scandalized was the Regency mama who learned of her precious son's consorting, and betting, with the *hoi polloi* at a cock fight or pugilistic display; in some gaming hells frequented by the gentry it took little more than a decently-tied cravat to get in the door, and even then standards might slip if enough gold weighed down a grimy purse. And while the tradition of a "debt of honor" has largely gone by the wayside now – a modern line of credit is enforced by more than just a threat of the cut direct – debts accrued to casinos and bookies and friendly neighborhood Pai gow parlors still break apart friendships, relationships, families and fortunes (as well as leading to corrupt police officers, as pretty much every crime thriller I have ever seen informs me).

Nevertheless, it seems to me that it is in the annals of Historical – mostly Georgian and Regency – Romance that we see gambling, and the concept of the inveterate gamester, played out most often even now (outside of, perhaps, anything set in Vegas), mostly because the denizens of the rarefied, moneyed heights in which we typically dwell rarely had anything better to do. They might not be addicts – especially not if they're our protagonists – and they might not even enjoy the undertaking, but by Jove, at least one of our characters must and will risk *something* (or everything) on the turn of a card because, as Heyer's young Hubert said so insightfully, *everyone* played.

Bet on it.

~HS~

**Rachel Hyland** is Editor of *Romantic Intentions Quarterly* and author of the Reading Heyer series, beginning with *Reading Heyer: The Black Moth*, released in 2018. Other non-fiction works include *Classics Gone Wild* (with Kate Nagy), *The White Queen: Reviewed* and *Project Film Geek*, among many more. She is a Heyer devotee to her very soul and 'pon rep, could not imagine life without all those brilliant, sparkling words. She lives in Melbourne, Australia. Also: lawks.

# 23.

# THE APPLE AND THE TREE: GEORGETTE HEYER, THE BLACK DAGGER BROTHERHOOD, AND THE ARISTOCRACY OF MERIT

## BY KATE NAGY

Georgette Heyer's influence is vast and continues to be felt among countless authors in numerous countries across multiple genres. In the introduction to her re-read of Heyer's works for Tor.com, Mari Ness notes an influence on romantic fantasy, particularly Patricia Wrede; and on the science fiction side, Lois McMaster Bujold has been vocal about Heyer's influence on her work, perhaps most famously in her "comedy of biology and manners," *A Civil Campaign.*[32]

But we can also catch unlikely echoes of Heyer in the genre of paranormal romance, broadly defined here as romantic fiction incorporating elements (particularly characters) whose existence in the physical world is, at best, a matter of conjecture and dispute. Vampires, shifters, zombies, mages, and angels (don't @me, faith-based reader friends) populate the pages of these books, which are particularly popular among younger readers.[33]

Here I will discuss Heyer's reach into the world of paranormal romance by way of a discussion of J.R. Ward's long-running, best-selling Black Dagger Brotherhood (BDB) series. Ward sets her paranormal fiction (she also writes general fiction and, occasionally, category romance) in a world with some striking similarities to Heyer's, particularly with respect to social structure. But after

---

[32] Nikohl K. and John Lennard, ed. *A Reader's Companion to* A Civil Campaign *by Lois McMaster Bujold: Compiled and Presented to Her by Members of the Official LMB Mailing-List to Celebrate the Silver Anniversary of Shards of Honor, 1986-2011.*

[33] Defined as readers ages 34 and under. Data from a survey of 2000 romance readers commissioned by the Romance Writers of America from NPD Book, 2017.

building a universe that parallels Heyer's (with, okay, more explicitly-rendered sex and bloodshed), Ward proceeds to systematically remove the underpinnings of that world. In this way, Ward's BDB novels simultaneously serve as a celebration of and a rebuke to Heyer's world of glittering rich folk having adventures. The first BDB novel, *Dark Lover*, was first published in 2005, and establishes the insular community of Caldwell, New York, where vampires and humans live side-by-side, although the humans are, for the most part, blissfully unaware of their midnight-dwelling neighbors. The vampire race is led by its lonely, bitter King, Wrath, who also leads a small group of the race's protectors, the Black Dagger Brotherhood—highly trained and deadly vampire warriors who do battle nightly against de-souled vampire slayers known as *lessers*. (When they're not out clubbing, that is. They do a lot of that, mostly in the early books. Ward:Club ZeroSum::Heyer:Almack's. Discuss.)

Anyway, Wrath crosses paths with a half-human woman, Beth Randall, who doesn't realize that her deceased father Darius was himself a Black Dagger Brother, making Beth half-vampire. Her ignorance of her own nature is dangerous, as she is poised to make the transition to full-on vampire-hood, at which point her life will change dramatically—she'll require regular blood meals to survive, among other things. In bringing Beth up to speed about what to expect in her new life, Wrath falls in love with her. Too bad he's already married...

The subsequent volumes of the series (which has attracted quite the cult following) relate the stories of the other Brothers, along with other individuals in the Brothers' orbit. Meanwhile, the Brothers face down various threats from within and without. Along the way, there's a lot of conspicuous consumption, loud rap music, posturing, gore, and white-hot vampire lovin'. Overall, the effect is about as far from Heyer's genteel Regency as you can possibly get without time bending time back on itself and paradoxically returning you to the loving embrace of Prinny et al.

But let's take a closer look.

First of all, both authors are justly celebrated for their careful world-building. Heyer's readers follow her characters into ballrooms, carriages, and well-appointed gardens, and in Heyer's Regency—

consistent with what we know about the early 19th century—social interactions are governed by a complex set of rules, both spoken and unspoken. Notably, Heyer, who died in 1974, never experienced Regency England directly; rather, her books reflect scrupulous research and painstaking devotion to detail, but her Regency is probably as much an artificial construct as is Ward's Caldwell, New York.

Ward, for her part, isn't constrained by the historical record, so she's free to take certain liberties. At the same time, her world, like Heyer's, is guided by strict rules (which admittedly sometimes get broken) and clearly defined rituals. For example, even as the Regency wedding might involve scrambling for a special license and rushing to book St. George's, the vampire wedding involves having the female's name carved on the male's back. And salt rubbed in. (I'd rather go for the special license, myself.) Ward has created specific and believable rituals for punishment (the *rythe*), for vengeance (*Ahvenging*), for funerals, and so on. If those rituals are bloodier and more intense... well, Ward is primarily writing paranormal romance, where "bloody" and "intense" are pretty much the author's tickets for admission.

Regency England has been described as "a devil-may-care world of low morals and high fashion,"[34] and while I wouldn't dare comment on Ward's characters' morality, I will note that Ward spills *a lot* of ink describing the Brothers' designer suits. Ward and Heyer also write heroes that are so similar that it's almost surprising, given that one deals with wealthy bloodsuckers and the other with vampires. (I'M SORRY, okay, I had to.) Discussing *The Black Moth*, Ness notes: "For Heyer fans...what makes this book fascinating is the first appearance of a character who would become, with various twitches here and there, her stock in trade: the wealthy, bored, indifferent, rude and often cruel male aristocrat (always, but always, wealthy) who cares little for society's pretensions (while upholding them), or, in other words, Heyer's version of a Byronic hero, but one with the ability to quip."

---

[34] Saul David, *Prince of Pleasure: The Prince of Wales and the Making of the Regency,* Little, Brown, 1998.

That sounds suspiciously like many of Ward's heroes, who are nearly always, if not rich, then at least *extremely* comfortable, and who spend a lot of their free time pushing the heroines away, at least initially. I know: Not All Black Dagger Brothers. (Butch, notably, digs Marissa's chill from the get-go. And Torhment and Autumn are friends, until they start insulting each other prior to finally mating.) But it's a fairly consistent pattern. Look at Zsadist, who is consistently mean to Bella even as he pines for her, for example.

It's no surprise that Bella is a member of the vampire aristocracy, the *glymera,* which Ward explicitly compares to the Regency *ton* in the Glossary of Terms that precedes each of the BDB books. But what is the aristocracy to Ward, really? I'm going to argue that in the BDB books, the term as we commonly understand it connotes two different, although related, things. One is the *glymera,* of course, which kind-of-sort-of includes the King and the First Family, although the First Family (and the Brotherhood, for that matter) appears to exist outside of the *glymera.*

It's significant, and I would argue highly significant, that unlike Heyer's joyful aristocrats, the *glymera* is moribund, hidebound, and living largely in the past. They go so far as to attempt to use Xcor and his Band of Bastards to oust Wrath as King. In fact, Ward, who obviously holds considerable affection for her creations, doesn't seem to particularly like the *glymera* as a group. As Ehlena muses in *Lover Avenged,* the *glymera* constitute "...the highest level of vampire civilian society, the arbiters of taste, the bastion of civility...and the cruelest enclave of know-it-alls on the planet, capable of making Manhattan muggers look like people you'd rather have in for dinner." And Marissa—largely self-exiled from the group after her brother self-righteously throws her out of the house, placing her in mortal danger, when she throws in her lot with the Brother Butch—frequently reflects on their cruelty, double standards, and general uselessness to society.

Apart from the *glymera,* however, there's an aristocracy of merit that seems to be coalescing around King Wrath and his family. Now, the BDB is already pretty high up in Caldwell's social pecking order, but under Wrath, membership in the Brotherhood is opening up to anyone who can make it through the training. This means aristocrats like Peyton and Paradise, whom we meet in the Black Dagger Legacy

141

spin-off series, are eligible to join, but so are commoners like Blaylock and Craeg. So are Butch, whose murky half-human lineage is something of a scandal, and Qhuinn, who was ejected from the *glymera* because—among other reasons—his mismatched eyes don't meet *glymera* standards for physical beauty.

In this new aristocracy, being part of the *glymera* doesn't necessarily give you an edge, but it doesn't disqualify you, either. Bella and Marissa are both aristocrats, as are the King's two principal advisors (aside from his half-human Queen), Abalone and Saxton; but Mary and Jane are human; Manny, like Butch, is half-human; and Vishous and Payne are the children of literal deities. On the other hand, Saxton's mate, Rhun, is a working man; Blaylock, the Brother Qhuinn's mate, likewise; and no one seems to know quite where John Matthew came from. Xcor is very definitely not an aristocrat, but his mate, Layla, is one of the Chosen—like the BDB, someone who exists outside the system, but she's no commoner, that's for sure.

Also, significantly, our heroes stand up to the *glymera* and their strictures at every turn. In *Lover Revealed,* Marissa single-handedly blocks an attempt to place all *glymera* females in *sehclusion,* a form of house arrest, "for their own safety"—an attempt supported by her own brother, it's worth noting. Paradise, daughter of the First Advisor to the King, defies her upbringing (although not her open-minded father) and takes commoner Craeg as her mate. And—most of all—at the end of *The King,* Wrath abolishes the monarchy, abdicates the throne, and is subsequently elected King-for-Life in a free and fair election.

"Abalone led the effort, and all those commoners you helped cast the votes. Every single one of them. You have been chosen by your people to lead," Beth tells him. "You are the King." Deeply moved, Wrath accepts the charge laid upon him, and in the subsequent books is seen to be interacting with commoners to an extent that would have been unheard of in previous generations. "Who knows," Wrath says of his son, Little Wrath. "Maybe he'll decide to run [for King]. But it will be his choice. Not a burden—and no one, from any segment of society, will be able to tell him that the female he chooses isn't worthy. *Ever.*"

Of course, Ward's writing doesn't map perfectly on to Heyer's. Heyer wrote clean, PG-rated novels; Ward never met a kink she didn't enthusiastically endorse. Heyer was funny on purpose; Ward may show flashes of humor here and there, but she's not deliberately *funny*, although if you can encounter characters named "Zsadist," "Rhage," "s'Ex," and "Manuel 'Manny' Manello, M.D.," without at least cracking a smile, you're a better, or at least more respectful, person than I. And I'll be the first to admit that some of Ward's more recent pairings—I'm thinking specifically of Qhuinn/Blaylock and Saxton/Rhun here—would possibly cause the conservative and old-school Heyer to clutch her pearls and run screaming into the night.

But if all literature is an enormous, long-running conversation in which authors speak to one another across time and space about things that matter, the two authors are definitely on speaking terms. Ward acknowledges the structure of Heyer's Regency, reflects it back, and then dismantles and rebuilds it. She recognizes both the allure and the pitfalls of a functional aristocracy of birth, and she also salutes the aristocracy of merit, in which characters of good faith— half-human, empath, working-class, gay, angel, or warrior—can rise in the King's esteem, regardless of background or birth. And while the two writers admittedly hail from different countries, time periods, and cultural milieus—Heyer revered the aristocracy, where as in Ward's America we can log on to the internet and read snarky commentary when the Duchess of Cambridge wears a navy dress to a garden party—Heyer is clearly one of Ward's literary progenitors.

The apple, it seems, doesn't fall far from the tree.

*~HS~*

Kate Nagy likes: home repair, thunderstorms, 80s references, and the *Lost* finale. Dislikes: home repair, big crowds, bad music, and the Joker in any incarnation. She writes for *Romantic Intentions Quarterly* and is the co-author of *Classics Gone Wild*. Her first novel, *White Rock Hill*, is forthcoming, and *Grandma's Secret Bookshelf: Re-Reading the Popular Women's Fiction of Yesteryear* will be released in Spring, 2019.

# 24.

# WAS GEORGETTE HEYER A SNOB, AND DOES IT MATTER?

## BY TABETHA WAITE

In my debut novel, *Why the Earl is After the Girl,* the Earl of Rockford accuses Miss Athena Hawthorne of stealing a priceless family brooch. She is the common-born daughter of a jeweler, and when left destitute, she is forced to accept an offer from a stranger to work as a governess. Eventually, she becomes a Countess, without a single drop of noble, or barely respectable, blood flowing through her veins.

This story has been rather well received since its publication in 2016—but it is hardly one that would have been approved by Georgette Heyer.

While celebrated around the globe for her contribution to the historical romance genre, more particularly that of the Regency era, it can't be denied that there is a noticeable lack of lower-class main characters in any of her historical novels. It makes a reader wonder: didn't Heyer believe a heroine outside of the gentry had as much right to a happy ending as a duke's daughter or an earl's sister, or even a General's niece? Or was it simply that these less blessed-by-birth characters were not, then, key selling points in a successful story?

It's no secret that the romance industry has changed over the years. It has evolved into something that takes on real world issues, which earlier books and authors did not. Same-sex couples, open and descriptive bedroom scenes, class struggles, social justice, political upheaval, and women's rights have all become hot topics in romantic fiction, especially in the historical genre. But this was not so in Heyer's time. So the question becomes: does omitting the story of a true common born heroine, or hero (even in *These Old Shades*, it turns out that the guttersnipe Léonie was the baby-swapped daughter of a Comte, and therefore acceptable to the Duke of Avon), who finds love in Regency society, mean Georgette Heyer was a snob?

Perhaps.

But perhaps with good reasons. For one, Heyer looked to Jane Austen as a role model—another celebrated author who wrote about families from the gentry. Certainly, Austen wrote of couples who were from different levels of society (Lizzy is below Mr. Darcy in social standing, as he is quick to point out), but Austen made it very clear that a marriage between different classes was a very bad idea. (eg. Mr. and Mrs. Bennet.)

Another reason may very well be that many of her novels were released during both the Great Depression and World War II. During that time, people were looking for a better life and searching for something positive to cling to. She gave them this by allowing her readers a glimpse into a luxurious past with her descriptive details of another era.

Yet another reason could simply be Heyer's own high standards and stern moral code. She was a respected and intelligent woman, in many ways ahead of her time. She was an Englishwoman, well-born and bred, and that station in life was what appealed to her. She did not write about other cultures, and she did not want her characters to be distressingly without means.

The truth is, whether or not Georgette Heyer was indeed a snob, she was undoubtedly a talented writer who wrote about what she knew. Love her or disagree with her, no one can deny that she laid a strong foundation for the thousands of Regency novels to follow, and she should be treated with nothing but respect for all she achieved in her long and successful career.

Her works have rightfully withstood the test of time—for all that the times have changed so very much.

*~HS~*

Tabetha **Waite** is an award-winning author of historical romance. She lives in Missouri with her husband and two daughters. She appreciates Georgette Heyer because of her knowledge of the Regency period and her influence on the modern romance novel.

# 25.

# HEYER'S HEIRS – WHAT TO READ AFTER GEORGETTE?

## BY AMANDA JONES

Georgette Heyer was born in 1902, which for some reason seems astonishing, I think because she still feels so very present by virtue of her work. Her last completed novel, *Lady of Quality*, was published in 1972, when I was twelve years old. By my mid-teens, I had read pretty much all she had written that could be easily purchased or borrowed from libraries. And thanks to books called *The Private World of Georgette Heyer,* and *Georgette Heyer's Regency England*, I also wanted to own hardcovers with dust wrappers by Arthur Barbosa.

Do you happen to remember second-hand book collecting in the 1970s? This is something that the internet has changed forever, but internet buying, whilst perhaps easily providing the object so avidly sought, can in no way replicate that surge of adrenalin as you walk in the door of a second-hand bookshop, nor that moment of complete happiness when you spy a much wanted title on the shelves before you. Then there were the family holidays when a long drive up or down the coast to your destination had to be punctuated by visits to all the little country towns in between because you never knew what you might find on the shelves of their local book- or charity shop.

In the 1970s and 80s in Australia, I predominantly owned the paperbacks published by Pan but there have been various reissues of Heyer's novels, some with a "look" more appropriate than others; right up until some quite ill-advised pastel covers in 2016.

One good thing arising from these various reissues is that it brings Heyer to a wider audience, particularly in the US, where she has been less consistently published. A bit sadly though, by virtue of those same covers, she has become firmly entrenched in the Romance section of most bookshops. Her work had many contemporary male admirers, but is now little read by men. However, I am pleased to note that one of my local stores shelves her in the General Fiction section, where it is slightly more likely that the casual male browser may happen upon her. So a big shout out to all the male Heyer readers, who share their enthusiasm with that famous Renaissance man, Stephen Fry.

But anyway, back to my teenage years in the 70s. The time came when I had read and re-read Georgette Heyer and Jane Austen and I wanted to find more books like those. I admit I read the nefarious Barbara Cartland – in my defense, she was prolific and everywhere, her books were very cheap and they were set during that lovely Regency period, about which so much was familiar (and surprise, surprise, we know why that was!). But once I had read two of her most obvious rips offs of Georgette Heyer, I had had enough.

So the search continued. I read the books of Clare Darcy, Marion Chesney (also known as M. C. Beaton), Alice Chetwynd Ley and others. Some of them are still being reissued today, or are being published for the first time electronically.

But ah, those innocent times of 60s and 70s Regency Romance. An oft-made comment is that in the 1970s, the bedroom door was flung open never to close again. The "bodice ripper" entered the lexicon, spearheaded by American author Kathleen Woodiwiss. Covers became filled with bare and rippling male chests, or semi draped, provocatively posed females with bosoms spilling out of their extraordinarily low necklined dresses, a tradition that continues to this very day. Arthur Barbosa they are not!

Heyer herself has never stopped selling, but the Regency Romance, of which she has been variously described as the Queen, Mother and Grandmother, has branched and morphed, whilst rarely losing sight of its debt to her. As noted on a blog post at Austen Prose[35], her novels and her heroes "...appealed to the romance reading audience to such an extent that they have been copied, revised and expanded upon... for almost a century."

Some writers capture the feel of the period better than others and have forged big reputations. There was a bit of a Regency boom in the 1990s and early 2000s, after so many years of over-the-top bodice

---

[35] Laurel Ann, www.austenprose.com, "Heyer's Heroes: Immutable Romance Archetypes," 31 August 2010.

147

rippers, and many of today's bestselling authors in the genre started out around that time with books that were a little more Heyer-like, although their later books are more modern interpretations of Regency. Which means those bedroom doors are, again, open very wide.

The high name recognition and bestselling power of some of these writers has been used at times to relaunch Heyer novels in the United States, and to introduce her name to readers to whom it is unknown. Interestingly, writer Janet Evanovich had not read Heyer but cites the influence of Amanda Quick on her characters Stephanie and Joe, from her Stephanie Plum series, saying they were straight out of a Regency – sort of Heyer, but one level removed.

One of the main bones of contention over time has been about the amount of sex, of varying levels of explicitness, included in the modern Regencies. Some say publishers wanted to keep the subgenre afloat and the books selling by appealing to a new generation of readers through the inclusion of more bedroom scenes (although I would have to say bedrooms seem to be rarely involved – balconies, gardens, carriages, and all sort of other uncomfortable places are often preferred). Others, like bestselling romance author Anne Gracie, have asserted that the genre is broad enough to cater for all preferences. Although I think you do have to work a little harder if you want to find the ones that stop with the kiss.

I have to confess I fall on the less is best end of the spectrum. Heyer's books may end with the happy union of hero and heroine, but this is generally achieved, as novelist Kate Fenton rather alliteratively puts it, "not by lightning bolts of lust but by liking and laughter"[36].

So where DO we turn when we want to read "more books like Georgette Heyer"? Recommendations can take us in all sorts of unanticipated directions, because we read and enjoy Heyer for different things. What is it that we love so much about Heyer that we must go looking for more such works?

Here are just a few of the factors that make up a Georgette Heyer novel, and therefore a satisfying Heyer substitute:

---

[36] Kate Fenton, "I've read her books to ragged shreds." *The Telegraph,* 29 July 2002.

- Accurately researched period setting
- Witty dialogue
- Wide canvas of relationships, characters and communities
- Ready sense of the ridiculous
- Quality prose! Sentences! Paragraphs!
- Meeting of minds, not just four bare legs in a bed
- Charm
- Happy endings
- Excellent plots

Like many of her fans, when I had read all of Georgette Heyer's books, I went looking for similar authors. I have read a lot of those currently writing in the Regency and historical genres, and enjoyed many of them, particularly the earlier novels before, dare I say it, some became a little formulaic, or overly laden with scenes of the instant chemistry type. Being formulaic is not an issue for those who like to know what to expect (and these days that does pretty much describe me). But even though Heyer herself, knowing the tastes of her reading public, described her own work as "the mixture as before" and despite the prevalence of her Mark I and Mark II heroes, the variety amongst her novels frees her of this charge.

The first sort of sideways move I made while looking for more like Heyer was into the crime genre. Long an admirer of (predominantly English) police procedurals, I gradually discovered writers in the 2000s whose stories were set in that familiar world of Regency England, and most of them are still, albeit not quickly enough, adding to their series. Some of those I have particularly enjoyed are the Sebastian St Cyr novels by C. S. Harris, the novels of Imogen Robertson, the Dido Kent stories by Anna Dean, and the Alec Halsey mysteries by Lucinda Brant. There is often a romantic subplot to these books that develops as the series moves on (and I do like a good series, where characters grow and change). But they are different enough, particularly in genre, that you don't feel let down if they don't measure up to Georgette. (Heyer herself, of course, also wrote crime, but those novels are part of the Golden Age, alongside her contemporaries Sayers, Allingham and Christie.)

So, Crime I already knew and enjoyed; it was no great stretch to slide into Historical Crime. But my next discovery was totally out of the blue: Science Fiction.

In Lois McMaster Bujold's *A Civil Campaign*, her dedication reads: "For Jane, Charlotte, Georgette and Dorothy – long may they rule." How can you resist a dedication like that?

*A Civil Campaign* was not the first of Bujold's books I read, but it is a pivotal book in the story of Miles Vorkosigan and resounds with Heyer echoes, although I wouldn't recommend starting with it as the story arc builds over several books. Cordelia, Aral and Miles take hold of you and do not let you go.

A common concept in writing, particularly in Sci-Fi and Fantasy, is that of worldbuilding, and Heyer's Regency England is a world with a surprisingly strong influence on contemporary Fantasy writing. Several writers have mentioned a love of Heyer or her dialogue, and others have created worlds of their own filled with magic and magicians, based on Jane Austen, but containing more than a touch of Heyer. The classic example is perhaps Patricia Wrede's 1991 novel *Mairelon the Magician* and its sequel *Magician's Ward*, both of which use several Heyer staples: a cross-dressing heroine, a London season, Regency language and personalities and witty dialogue. These are two of my favorite books, and I defy anyone to read the end of *Mairelon the Magician* without it calling to mind those fabulous endings of *The Grand Sophy* or *The Unknown Ajax*, where one character gathers all the rest together, then orchestrates a successful denouement, creating order from chaos. They leave with the man or woman of their choice and we leave in fits of laughter.

Wrede herself has written quite a bit on what she calls crossover fiction, where one book deliberately mixes common tropes from two very different genres. Ideally it will expand the audience for both as some readers discover that they like whichever part of the crossover they don't normally read.

This was definitely my experience, although I have not really turned into a permanent reader of Sci-Fi or Fantasy (although I will note that Alison Goodman's Lady Helen series is also worth a look). Still, looking for "something like Georgette" can take us down some unexpected, but delightful and enjoyable paths.

Especially if you sidestep into non-fiction.

As many of her readers know, Georgette Heyer fiercely guarded her privacy and did not give interviews. Again, there was a time before the internet, and it was a time of scarcity of information about this beloved author.

One of the first critical appraisals of her work was A. S. Byatt's 1969 article "Georgette Heyer is a Better Novelist Than You Think," in which she wrote the oft-quoted line "Heyer is a superlatively good writer of honourable escape." But for most of Heyer's legion of admirers, it was not until obituaries were published that they learnt she was also Mrs. Ronald Rougier and had a husband, son and grandchildren.

Beautifully titled "The Ferocious Reticence of Georgette Heyer" was a 10-page supplement in the *Sunday Times* magazine in 1975, the year after her death, again written by Byatt. It was the first biographical portrait of Heyer, written with the co-operation of her husband and family, who provided photos and contacts with friends and publishers. It also included a longer critical appreciation of her work and of the extent of research in which she engaged to reach such high levels of historical accuracy and authenticity.

The first full-length Heyer biography was written by Jane Aiken Hodge. She wrote:

> *Should one now, almost ten years after Heyer's death, try and look behind the curtain of privacy in which she shrouded herself? My first instinct, when I started work on this book, was to concentrate entirely on the work, merely giving the barest facts of her life as a foreword. Then I began to talk to the people who knew her, and to read her letters. Everyone who knew her had loved or respected her, and they all seemed glad that a book should be written about her.*

The original hardcover edition is beautifully and lavishly illustrated and weaves the stories of her characters with the stories of her life. I was thrilled to buy a copy of this when it first came out, because reading about Heyer's novels, written by someone who obviously loved them too, was the next best thing to reading Heyer.

Teresa Chris's 1989 book *Georgette Heyer's Regency England* was next. She wrote in the introduction:

*Georgette Heyer created her own special Regency world based on an exact knowledge of the period (and) the settings of her world still exist - London, Brighton, Bath and other locations around England are rich in regency heritage and hence rich in memories for fans.*

I made extensive use of the book on a recent trip to London and Bath. I so wish Almack's Assembly Rooms was still there instead of Almack House the office block! I had a slightly surreal moment when I was in London – at the start of my trip, I was wandering around the St. James area with Theresa Chris in hand, looking at the men's clubs, and trying to imagine the dandies strolling, or, more excitingly *The Grand Sophy* in her dashing phaeton kidnapping Miss Wraxton so she could see the bow windows. But the amount of traffic was SO huge, a constant and almost unmoving stream of great big trucks, and cars and buses, that it was a little difficult to envisage what it must have been like. But when I returned to the capital at the end of my four-week drive through England (in the incessant rain), it coincided with a 10k run through the streets of London. There were absolutely no vehicles at all on St James St or along Piccadilly. It was much easier to populate the streets with horses and carriages, ladies shopping at Hatchards with its windows still filled with all the newest publications, and Beau Brummell and our many heroes, strolling around the corner from their clubs to Almack's to gain entry before the famed 11pm closing of the doors.

Another non-fiction book worth the reading for any Heyer fan is Mary Fahnestock-Thomas's *Georgette Heyer: A Critical Retrospective* (2001), an enjoyable collection to dip into and out of, including as it does some of Heyer's short stories, over one hundred reviews of her works, obituaries and various other articles.

And then there is Jennifer Kloester. I am sure I am not the only Heyer fan who wishes they'd had the idea to write a thesis on her work. To my knowledge, at least three people have created that opportunity for themselves, best-known of whom is Jennifer Kloester, whose Ph.D. research was put to use in the 2005 book *Georgette Heyer's Regency World*.

A review in the *Times Literary Supplement* described it as:

*A Heyer lover writing for Heyer fans ... From the fascinating slang, the elegant fashions, the precise ways the bon ton ate, drank, danced, and flirted, to the shocking real life scandals of the day,* Georgette Heyer's Regency World *takes you behind the scenes of Heyer's captivating novels.*

And then came Kloester's critically acclaimed biography, *Georgette Heyer* (2011). It builds significantly on the Hodge work, as Kloester had access to an amazing archive of Heyer's letters, private papers and notebooks, and was generously supported and encouraged by Heyer's son, Sir Richard Rougier.

So Heyer is now a recognized and legitimate subject of academic study. A cursory search unearths journal articles and lecture titles, as well as a unit on historical fiction that included *Henry V, Ivanhoe* and *Sylveste*r. There was also an English language-delivered 14-week course on Regency and desert romance in a German university, which included *Bath Tangle*, and there are papers with titles like "Intertextuality and *Venetia*," and "*The Nonesuch* as didactic love fiction."

The first Georgette Heyer conference was held at Lucy Cavendish College Cambridge in 2009. Academic in focus, it included papers on such topics as "Publishing Heyer: Representing the Regency in Historical Romance," "The Thermodynamics of Georgette Heyer: Variations on the Quest for Revitalisation," and "Cross-Dressing and Disguise in Heyer's Historical Romances."

Portions of this essay were, in fact, originally presented as a paper at a conference on Georgette Heyer in 2016, the second to be held in Sydney, since which time an interdisciplinary conference aimed primarily at exploring Heyer's historical novels was held in London in 2018, with other conferences in the planning stages, as of this writing.

So, after Georgette come many possibilities, guided by your taste, preferences and/or willingness to try new things. Fiction, non-fiction, scholarly, amateur, the options are tantalizing. But for me, they all lead back, again and again, to the nonpareil herself, Georgette Heyer.

*~HS~*

**Amanda Jones** has been involved in organizing two very successful Georgette Heyer conferences in Sydney, Australia, and is looking forward to a third in 2019. Having read *Pride and Prejudice* around age 12, and looking for someone to read who was like Jane Austen, Amanda was directed by a helpful school librarian to a whole shelf of books by Georgette Heyer. She has read them repeatedly over the ensuing decades whilst raising a family and working in a number of different fields, and they have never failed to lift her spirits.

# i.

# MY FIRST HEYER

## DONNA CUMMINGS

I am not 100% certain my first Heyer was *Venetia*, but it *feels* like it is. I started reading Georgette Heyer's books in the previous century, so certain details are bound to be lost to the passage of time, but this one left an indelible impression. A recent re-read reminded me how the literary style is definitely out of favor with current writing rules: No adverbs! No exclamation points! No long sentences! Thankfully that spare style of writing was not in vogue when I lost my heart to the "incurably candid" Venetia and her rakish, guilty pleasure hero, Lord Damerel. Who wouldn't fall in love with a man who "bore himself with a faint suggestion of swashbuckling arrogance," yet, after stealing a kiss, finds himself even more enchanted with Venetia's quick-witted retorts? And who could resist a heroine who brushes aside Damerel's offer to improve his shocking reputation with, "Oh no, we should have nothing to talk about any more!" Whether or not *Venetia* was my first Heyer, it is definitely a love story worth experiencing over and over again.

## JANGA

I first read Georgette Heyer back in the 60s when the media was filled with news of riots and protests and my generation was convinced that we were changing the world. I ran across *These Old Shades* in a bookstore where I was browsing for escapist reading. The story of Léonie and the Duke of Avon delighted me. I went back the next day and bought *Devil's Cub* and *A Convenient Marriage*, and I have been reading and rereading Heyer ever since.

## KIRSTEN ELLIOTT

In 1957 there was an Asian Flu epidemic in the United Kingdom. I escaped that one but when it returned in 1959, I was one of the children struck down. I was ill for weeks. My mother, faced with a bedridden, bored pre-teen was kept busy finding entertaining books for me to read. Among them was **Devil's Cub**.

This was a stroke of genius on my mother's behalf. For a start, being pale-skinned, hazel-eyed and dark-haired myself, unlike the then fashionable blue-eyed blondes with peaches and cream complexions, Mary Challoner was the perfect heroine for me. I was captivated when I read about her chestnut curls and cool grey eyes standing little chance compared with her sister Sophia's bright gold ringlets and limpid blue eyes. I was immediately on her side. Everything about her chimed with me, especially her rather studious nature, calm good sense and dry wit. Strangely, I was not so keen on Dominic Alastair, Marquis of Vidal. I considered him downright irritating at times. It was his father I found attractive. His polite sarcasm made me laugh out loud at times. I still inwardly chuckle over the exchange where Mary informs him why she shot Vidal. She explains that Vidal then saw she was in deadly earnest.

> *"Did he indeed? A gentleman of intuition, I perceive," the Duke of Avon dryly replies.*

Reading it again now, I realize this influenced my own style of humor forever. However, with the advent of the 1960s, bringing with them idols such as the Beatles, Rolling Stones and Bob Dylan, Heyer was definitely not cool. I did not read her again for many years, but now I appreciate her writing, her research, and her humor, not to mention her literary style, in ways that I did not then. In 1959, *Devil's Cub* was the perfect piece of escapism for an ailing schoolgirl, and I have never forgotten the pleasure it gave me.

## JENNIFER KLOESTER

The first Heyer novel I ever came across was **Cotillion**. My husband's grandmother had it in the glove compartment of her car and I remember pulling it out and being a little overwhelmed by the language. I next encountered a Heyer novel while living in Papua New Guinea. It was in the tiny YWCA library in Tabubil, a small mining town in the Star Mountains in PNG's Western Province. *These Old Shades* was like nothing I'd ever read before and it set me on a quest to read every Heyer novel I could find. Luckily, the library had a pretty good collection and whenever we flew back to Australia on leave I would scour the bookshops in search of more of her novels. Over time I amassed a nice collection of paperbacks – many of which I still own.

When we went to live in the Middle East I was amazed to discover an almost complete collection of Heyer novels in the town library. That's where I first read her contemporary novels and most of her historicals and detective stories. I vividly remember reading *Devil's Cub* in Bahrain and adoring Mary. She was so honest and courageous and I loved her determination in refusing to do what Dominic wanted. Mary had principles but she also had a sense of humor and could be romantic. I loved that combination. I must have read that book a dozen times.

I also learned to love *A Civil Contract* while living in the Middle East. I hadn't been so taken with the story when I'd first read it in New Guinea: it wasn't like Heyer's other novels and I'd always felt sorry for Jenny. When I read it in Bahrain I saw the story differently. I could see what Heyer saw – that Jenny and Adam's relationship was one based on friendship and that over time the love between them would grow into something much stronger and more lasting than the passion Adam had felt for Julia. One of the reasons Heyer's novels endure is that she understood human nature and was able to create living, breathing characters for whom her readers feel real a genuine emotional connection. As her readers grow and age, so their perceptions of Heyer's stories and characters also change. This is one of the hallmarks of a great writer.

**CLARA SHIPMAN**

My first Heyer was *Frederica*, and if there is a better way to get to know an author, I don't know what it is. *Frederica* is Heyer at the height of her power – funny, exciting, romantic, electric. The terminally selfish Marquis of Alverstoke turning over a new leaf for love of a good woman and her little brothers—it's the greatest redemption story in Heyer, and the perfect entry into her Regency domain. I still love *Frederica* to this day – I even named my dog Lufra!

**RUTH WILLIAMSON**

*The Talisman Ring* captivated my 13- or 14-year-old self instantly with its mysterious young heir under a cloud, his matter of fact cousin, the youthful French innocent, soon joined by a lady with a wicked sense of humor, and a smiling villain. The novel romped along at the pace of a bolting horse. I fell headlong for its romantic leads. Not only the impetuous young couple, but especially the brusque, mature male who encounters his match in a clever woman. In fact, the verbal sparring of this second pair stole the show. Interruptions to my absorption of this novel were, and remain, as unacceptable to me as an officer of the law curtailing the enjoyment of the best duty-free French Burgundy.

**KAREN ZACHARY**

I'm not sure what, or who, inspired me to read a Georgette Heyer romance, but just seven years ago, *Sylvester, or The Wicked Uncle* was my first, and I must admit that I did not love it. At that time, the only historical romances that I had read were by authors like Mary Stewart and Victoria Holt – back in my teenage years – so I was not prepared for Heyer's style. On second reading, however, I better appreciated the humor, characterization, and wonderful dialogue, and in the intervening years I have read or listened to *Sylvester* several times and count it among my favorites.

*~HS~*

# MY FAVORITE HEYER

## RACHEL HYLAND

I have gone into some depth elsewhere in this collection about my love of *Venetia*, and how it wasn't always my favorite Heyer novel – that title previously held by *Arabella* – but now most assuredly is. But I have other favorites! So many other favorites! Restricting myself to merely a Top 5, they are: 1) the aforementioned; 2) *These Old Shades*; 3) *Frederica*; 4) *Cotillion*; and 5) *Simon the Coldheart* (which I may also have mentioned in these pages). But this is always subject to change! There are at least fifteen of Heyer's fifty books that I would rank as among my favorite works of literature ever. So, what is my favorite Heyer? *Venetia*... for now. But tomorrow, who knows? It might be *Sprig Muslin*! Or *The Unknown Ajax*! Or *Cotillion*! Or *Friday's Child*!... or... or...

## JANGA

*Frederica* is my uncontested favorite Heyer. I love everything about it, from its determined heroine and cynical hero to the large cast of relatives, near and distant, who are part of their lives, each one a distinct personality. I am particularly fond of Frederica's young brothers, the scholarly Jessamy and the irrepressible Felix, and their dog Lufra, who is transformed into a rare Baluchistan hound. The abundance of romances is a plus, and Frederica's unconscious taming of the jaded Alverstoke, who finds he has a heart after all, is a story of which I never tire. In fact, just writing about it makes me eager for a reread.

## JENNIFER KLOESTER

An impossible question with an ever-changing answer, because anyone who knows Heyer's novels will agree that choosing a favorite – *one* favorite – cannot be done. But if I *had* to choose – I mean if I was being marooned on a desert island or had a gun to my head or if my library were threatened by fire or flood and I could save only one book then it would have to be... *Venetia*, or wait... *A Civil Contract*... No... *Friday's Child* or... what about *The Grand Sophy* or *The Talisman Ring* or *Frederica* or... Oh dear... All right, if I really *must* choose, then let it be **Sylvester**, a book that brilliantly showcases Heyer's wit and ironic humor, her eye for period detail, her sparkling dialogue, her complex characterization and her talent for creating clever plots. Best of all, *Sylvester* has one of her superb imbroglio endings which makes me laugh aloud whenever I read it. This is a novel rich in meaning and one which never fails to delight. Heyer's characters leap from the page as living, breathing people; they take the reader by the hand and draw them, smiling, into their story. There is deep emotion here and brilliant comedy and for those in the know, just the mention Sir Nugent Fotherby's name is enough to evoke a chuckle. So, if I may have only one of Georgette Heyer's wonderful novels, then let it be *Sylvester* and I shall while away the hours of my captivity with pleasure.

**CLARA SHIPMAN**

It's a hard call. I have favorites in each of Heyer's time periods, Medieval, Georgian, Regency, Contemporary. So I am going to list all four of them, try to make something of it, I dare you. My favorite of the Medieval novels is **Simon the Coldheart**, because Simon is awesome and the way he fixes up his castle is like the best home makeover show ever and because the other ones are *very* historical and so kind of dry. My favorite of the Georgian novels is **The Talisman Ring**, because Eustacie is adorable and Sir Hugh Thane is a boss. My favorite Regency is harder to pick, but I'm going to go with **Frederica**, because it just gets me every time, I could read it every day and never get bored. And my favorite of her contemporary novels is a mystery, **Why Shoot a Butler?** Because, yeah, why? I like that it has a kind of *Upstairs/Downstairs*, *Downton Abbey* vibe, way before either of those things existed.

**MAURA TAN**

It feels like a bit of a cheek, weighing in with my favorite Heyer novel when I have read all of four of them, and all four are the contemporary novels the author herself didn't like. But I've got to give **Pastel** some love, because it is a really good book and I've been thinking about it pretty consistently since I read it. The thing about *Pastel* is, as well as having some very entertaining scenes, it is also shot through with a brittle world-weariness and self-involved snarkiness that is just really, really *real*. I don't have to have read any of her historical romances to call it Heyer's *Vanity Fair*. This book should be better known. All Heyer fans should read it, at the least.

## KAREN ZACHARY

How can one choose a single favorite Georgette Heyer novel? But the editor asked the question, and my answer must be **Venetia**. I like that Venetia and Damerel are older than the typical Regency romance couple and that they actually talk to one another like adults. I adore the low-key humor, the literary allusions, Aubrey's quirky intelligence, and Damerel's downright sexiness (unique among Heyer heroes, in my opinion). I enjoyed every character in *Venetia*, from the awful Mrs. Scorrier to the annoying Edward Yardley to the rather adorable Sir Lambert Steeple. I have lost count of how many times I have read or listened to this book. Like Damerel, *Venetia* is my own "dear delight."

Having said all of this, I do think that *A Civil Contract* is Heyer's finest work, a book that deserves to be liberated from the "Regency romance" category and considered as serious fiction. It is not really even a romance, given that Adam and Jenny marry for money and nothing else. I realize that this book is not universally popular, but as a realistic and touching example of a 19th century *mariage de convenance,* it is excellent.

*~HS~*

# MY FAVORITE HEYER HERO

**RACHEL HYLAND**

With apologies to Waldo and Simon and Tristram, to Avon and Alverstoke and Damerel, my favorite Heyer hero is without a doubt **Freddy Standen**, of *Cotillion*. Why? Because Freddy is barely even his own hero, at the start of the novel, and by the end he has become everything we could want in a man—the kind of man he would never have had the hubris to believe he could be. When our action commences, the kindly Freddy just wants to (and/or, is persuaded to) do a good turn for his sweet, neglected almost-cousin, for whom he has always had a fondness. Kitty's plight sees him forced to draw on hidden depths to solve crises of varying degrees, all while being pleasant and decent and just a lovely, if occasionally frustrated by museums, human being. Freddy proves that it doesn't have to be all alpha males and love/hate witty barbs, it doesn't have to be esoteric quotes and sporting prowess and a thunderous brow. Sometimes, the swoonworthiest hero is the one who is just... really nice. (Special mention must go to Freddy's scene-stealing father, Lord Legerwood, and to the excellent Mr. Charles Trevor, private secretary to Lord Alverstoke of *Frederica*, both heroes in their own right.)

**JANGA**

I adore Gervase Frant, seventh Earl of St. Erth (*The Quiet Gentleman)* and the Honorable Frederick Standen *(Cotillion)*, but my favorite Heyer hero is **Major Hugo Darracott** of *The Unknown Ajax*. He has all the qualities I value most in a hero – intelligence, confident competence, and a killer sense of humor. I never tire of rereading the scene in which Hugo directs the Darracotts plus the valet Polyphant in saving young Richmond from the excisemen. It is not only deliciously funny, but it shows Hugo as a hero who can solve whatever problems arise.

**JENNIFER KLOESTER**

The choice of a favorite Heyer hero depends on the criteria. Does one want a romantic hero like Sir Anthony Fanshawe or Gervase Frant? Or a cynical, sardonic hero like the Duke of Avon or Miles Calverleigh? Perhaps an omniscient hero like Mr. Beaumaris or a dashing one like Beau Wyndham or a charming scapegrace like Anthony Sheringham? One of Heyer's great talents was her ability to create character and, while she sometimes referred to her "Mark I" or "Mark II" heroes, the truth is that her male leads are a diverse lot with no two being exactly alike. Each of her heroes is perfectly suited to his story and several times she made the hero the main focus of her novel (*Sylvester, The Unknown Ajax, False Colours, Charity Girl*).

For her readers, Heyer's heroes are living, breathing men who are attractive in very different ways. Though I love them, popular favorites such as Jasper Damerel and Dominic Alastair would not be my choice given that my personal preference is for kinder, more reliable men. Sir Tristram Shield for example, or that gentle giant, Hugo Darracott, or kind Freddy Standen. They are intelligent, modest men and they each have a sense of humor. I love Tristram for his integrity and strength of character, Hugo for his love of a joke, his quick-thinking and perception, and Freddy for his innate goodness, his retiring disposition and his hidden depths. To choose among these three is difficult but in the end I cannot go past **Hugo Darracott** of *The Unknown Ajax*, who as well as being amiable, charming and handsome also has at least half a million pounds to his name!

## CLARA SHIPMAN

It should be Simon, of *Simon the Coldheart*, because he is just badass all the way around, but my favorite Heyer hero is actually **Gilly Ware, the Duke of Sale** of *The Foundling*, a shy, sweet but suggestible soul who runs away from home to help his cousin but ends up helping a beautiful orphan of uncertain background—and falling in love with his own fiancé. Gilly is a sweetheart, and wins this round easily. Simon would take him in any other kind of fight, though, guaranteed.

## RUTH WILLIAMSON

*Black Sheep*'s eponymous black sheep, **Miles Calverleigh**, views Bath society and its hangers-on through heavy-lidded, cynical eyes. He sees the world from the perspective of experience of the school of life. From the moment this sallow-skinned, carelessly dressed and unconventional character appears on the page, he challenges assumptions about what underpins genteel behavior. His warm smile and sense of the ridiculous mitigate his eye to the main chance. He is a mature hero, unfashionable, and as much of a dark horse as he is a prodigal son. His exchanges with the heroine, Abby Wendover, are punctuated by wit, humor and fellow feeling. In fact, when he is absent from any scene, it is the poorer for lacking his undeniable charm. For all that, he has his faults. A distinct lack of polished drawing room manners marks his sharp contrast with a Heyer hero like Mr. Robert Beaumaris. Yet Miles Calverleigh overstates the case when he tells Abby that he has no virtues: he proves fully capable of rescuing his chosen lady from her particular silken cage. His strategy is masterly, in keeping with his business acumen. His wife will be a very fortunate lady.

**KAREN ZACHARY**

**Freddy Standen**, the unlikely hero of *Cotillion*, holds a special place in my heart. At first, we think he is just another overdressed pink of the ton and none too bright. As the story unfolds, however, we see that Freddy is a good-hearted, stand-up fellow who cheerfully goes about extricating Kitty from the various fixes she gets herself into. Early in the book handsome, charming Jack looks to be the hero, but Freddy has depths that are not apparent at first, and by the end it is Freddy that fills that spot. I can't think of another Heyer where the ultimate hero is so well concealed. I found him just adorable.

*~HS~*

# MY FAVORITE HEYER HEROINE

### RACHEL HYLAND

My devotion to *Frederica*, to *Venetia*, to *Pen* and *Sarah* and *Léonie* know no bounds, but my very favorite Heyer heroine is without a doubt **Mistress Prudence Tremaine**, aka Mr. Peter Merriot, of *The Masqueraders*. Here is a woman forced to disguise herself as a man, and carry herself as one too, in order to keep her brother safe from prosecution after a treasonous uprising. Here is a woman of wit, ingenuity and acumen, skillful with a sword and with a dice box, wholly at home in the company of men at a time when that was a feat considered nigh on impossible. The fact that Prue finds her true love while in disguise – with a man eventually perspicacious enough to see through the façade to the woman beneath – is a testament to her many talents.

### JANGA

Choosing a favorite Heyer heroine is difficult since I have a great fondness for all her active heroines who don't hesitate to take matters into their own capable hands. Certainly, the delightful Sophia Stanton-Lacey (*The Grand Sophy*), who sets to right a whole family plus assorted hangers-on, is a contender, as is witty Venetia Lanyon who proves a match for all the "wiser heads" who try to separate her from Damerel. But **Frederica Merriville** of *Frederica* edges them out for top favorite. Her devotion to her siblings, her sense of responsibility to them, and her conviction that she knows best for them resonates strongly with me, also an eldest child. And I love her audacity in assigning ownership of Lufra, the cow-stampeding canine to the Marquis of Alverstoke.

### JENNIFER KLOESTER

It's not easy choosing a favorite heroine from one of Georgette Heyer's many novels – there are so many obvious candidates: Sophy,

Léonie, Venetia, Frederica, Arabella, Mary Challoner, Sarah Thane, Drusilla Morville, Anthea Darracott – all of them deserve their popularity, but my choice is for a heroine often overlooked, both by her readers and by her fictional friends and family. She is a woman constrained by the rules and etiquette of her time, a woman forced to stifle her intellect and to hide it behind a camouflage of docility. Yet she is smart and funny and, despite the dismal reality of her situation in life, she is a woman who maintains her integrity with a ferocity belied by her shyness and soft-speaking. Those around her are mostly blind to the real woman and recognize neither her sense of humor nor her capacity for love. Kind, honorable and perceptive, **Hester Theale** from *Sprig Muslin* is one of Heyer's finest characters – a woman of immense courage and unexpected spirit. Complex and surprising, she is fully realized in the novel as a three-dimensional character with a depth of feeling that continues to surprise readers. Hester has never failed to intrigue me and the scene where she hides behind the curtain in Sir Gareth's bedchamber is one of Heyer's funniest. Hester is the sister I always wished I'd had.

**CLARA SHIPMAN**

Is there even a more perfect heroine in all of fiction than *The Grand Sophy*'s **Sophia Stanton-Lacy**? That book is problematic to a modern audience, of course, but none of it can be blamed on Sophy. She is a whirlwind, a force of nature, the kind of heroine you just can't help but adore, and wish to be. She is Emma, except she doesn't attempt to sort out people's lives because it makes her feel important, she does it because she wants everyone to be happy and she has the power to make that happen. Sophy is especially notable for the way she takes some of the silly, not to mention misogynist, conventions of the time and makes them her bitch. Her eventual romance with her cousin I can take or leave (I would rather have seen her end up with Sir Vincent), but there is something appealing about their love/hate thing, as well. Sophy deserved better than Charles, but Charles could never have done better than Sophy. She is my total Regency girlcrush.

**RUTH WILLIAMSON**

*The Reluctant Widow's* **Elinor Rochdale** has seen more of the world than another personal favorite, Jane Austen's Elinor Dashwood. Both heroines are level-headed women of sense, who face up to the consequences of family financial losses. For Heyer's Elinor, there is the added sting of having been jilted. She has become a governess to support herself and arrives at dilapidated Highnoons in Sussex to take up a new position. It is not the highly unusual one offered by Edward, Lord Carlyon, the autocratic peer she meets there, who is definitely not Austen's diffident Edward Ferrars. Elinor Rochdale has an independent turn of mind. This gives rise to spirited discussions with his lordship. Overnight she becomes a widow and the chatelaine of Highnoons, where she encounters (amongst others) an impetuous adolescent, a series of highly suspect "visitors," and a raw-boned canine. Soon she transforms Lord Carlyon's original idea of her potential. Free-spirited Elinor enjoys provoking him by challenging any and all of his advice. Furthermore, she acts courageously and proves to be a capital whip. In her vivacity she differs from Austen's Elinor. The reluctant widow is not only resourceful and quick-witted, she is lively. This makes her irresistible, and my favorite among Heyer's heroines.

## KAREN ZACHARY

Without doubt, **Frederica Merriville** is my favorite heroine. Indeed *Frederica* is a close second as my favorite of all of Heyer's romances. Like my beloved Venetia, she is older than many Regency heroines. (Are you seeing a pattern here? Can you guess that I'm no spring chicken?) Frederica is a no-nonsense woman but so full of love for her family that she has devoted herself to them at the expense of her own potential marital happiness. I adore her modesty and wit and patience. How could Alverstoke help but want to give her everything he has? Indeed, I think Alverstoke fell in love with the entire Merriville clan. I know that I did.

*~HS~*

# V.

# MY LEAST FAVORITE HEYER

## RACHEL HYLAND

When first pondering this question, I immediately thought for sure, *Cousin Kate*. No question. But then I really considered it and I realized... you know, Heyer's historical fiction outings are, by and large, my least favorite of her works, and the one of those I have always found it most difficult to get through, and that has stuck with me the least over the years, is ***Royal Escape***. I kind of forget it exists, even, so I went to read it again just to make sure. And yes, it does exist, and it's... not great. Oh, it is no doubt extremely historically accurate, as meticulously researched as are all of Heyer's works, and it does have its good points—notably, the deposed King Charles II's time on a peasant farm, learning to be common folk. But for a novel about a beautiful young man's desperate escape to avoid beheading at the hands of ruthless usurpers (there is no doubt where Heyer's loyalties lie, and it is definitely with the Crown), it is all rather dull, really. The fact is, I'd rather reread *Cousin Kate* than reread *Royal Escape*. And that is saying *a lot*.

## JANGA

Most Heyer books, even those that rank low on my list of Heyers to reread, feature characters that capture my interest and affection. ***The Reluctant Widow*** is that rare Heyer creation – a book whose characters bore me. When I consider how much I dislike *The Reluctant Widow,* I remind myself that even Shakespeare had his *Titus Andronicus.*

## JENNIFER KLOESTER

This is a tricky question, as to name a least favorite Heyer might imply that there is a book of hers I do not like – well, there is one I'm not fond of, but *My Lord John* was her only posthumous novel and the only book she never actually finished writing, so I'm not sure it really counts. To pick a least favorite I've had to consider the Heyer novels I re-read least often. There's only a handful among the historicals: *Bath Tangle, April Lady, Cousin Kate* and *Charity Girl*. Of these, probably **Charity Girl** is the one I rarely re-read. Though I find Viscount Desford's quest to save Cherry Steane mildly entertaining, the account of his travels about the country trying to find her grandfather and resolve her situation tends to distract from the real story of Des and Hetty's relationship. I do love the language, however, much of which is new and some of which is utterly entertaining in its own right ("You're a skitterbrain, sir! A slibberslabber here-and-thereian"). This is a slighter book than Heyer's usual rich offering and has less of her brilliant comedy and this was undoubtedly due to her poor health. Her years of smoking had begun to take their toll and writing was becoming increasingly difficult for her. I do enjoy the final chapters of *Charity Girl* and I'd love Heyer to have written Simon's story but this was to be her second-last book, and though not a favorite there is still enough Heyer in it to make it worth reading.

**CLARA SHIPMAN**

There are a few I'll probably never read again (*Cousin Kate, The Conqueror, April Lady*) but the only book of Georgette Heyer's I actively dislike is **The Spanish Bride**. I first read it when I was sixteen, and Juana, the book's heroine, is only fourteen, and she *gets married* and then "falls in love" with the man who basically takes advantage of her need to be rescued from gang rape. And it is heavily implied that the only reason she deserves to be spared such horror is because she is from the Castilian class, while all around them women everywhere are being abused horribly by English and allied soldiers, but that's okay, because they don't wear mantillas. As an accurate portrayal of the horrors of war (and this is based on a true story, which Heyer could hardly help) I can applaud the book, but for the way it romanticizes Juana's plight, is kind of mean about Spanish people, and tries to make Harry a saint, when actually a 25-year-old man taking an orphaned teenager to his bed is all kinds of wrong, it just makes me angry every time I think about it.

**KAREN ZACHARY**

***The Grand Sophy*** is one of Heyer's most popular books and the favorite of many fans. Please don't throw things at me, but I can't stand it, primarily because I can't stand Sophy. She is ill-mannered, arrogant and bossy, considering herself the expert at deciding what is good for everyone else. As for the story itself, I find it weak, filled with unappealing, two-dimensional characters. Sophy meddles in everyone else's romances, and then finds love herself (not until virtually the final page) with her stuffy, overbearing cousin who tells her flat out that he can't stand her. Bah! I really cannot see a happily ever after coming from this match.

Moreover, the entire ending is too over-the-top for me. It is one of what Jennifer Kloester calls Heyer's "imbroglio endings," which remind me too much of Hollywood's 1930s screwball comedies. Simply not to my taste. I will admit, however, that I do love the "imbroglio ending" of *The Unknown Ajax*, but perhaps that's because I found Hugo delightful and love how he stage-managed the final scenes with most of the crowd being none the wiser.

*~HS~*

# GEORGETTE HEYER'S BIBLIOGRAPHY

**Georgian Novels**

*The Black Moth* (Constable, 1921)
*The Transformation of Philip Jettan,* aka *Powder and Patch* (Mills & Boon, 1923)
*These Old Shades* (William Heinemann, 1926)
*The Masqueraders* (William Heinemann, 1928)
*Devil's Cub* (William Heinemann, 1932)
*The Convenient Marriage* (William Heinemann, 1934)
*The Talisman Ring* (William Heinemann, 1936)
*Faro's Daughter* (William Heinemann, 1941)

**Regency Novels**

*Regency Buck* (William Heinemann, 1935)
*An Infamous Army* (William Heinemann, 1937)
*The Spanish Bride* (William Heinemann, 1940)
*The Corinthian* (William Heinemann, 1940)
*Friday's Child*(William Heinemann, 1944)
*The Reluctant Widow* (William Heinemann, 1946)
*The Foundling*(William Heinemann, 1948)
*Arabella* (William Heinemann, 1949)
*The Grand Sophy* (William Heinemann, 1950)
*The Quiet Gentleman* (William Heinemann, 1951)
*Cotillion* (William Heinemann, 1953)
*The Toll-Gate* (William Heinemann, 1954)
*Bath Tangle* (William Heinemann, 1955)
*Sprig Muslin* (William Heinemann, 1956)
*April Lady* (William Heinemann, 1957)
*Sylvester, or the Wicked Uncle* (William Heinemann, 1957)
*Venetia* (William Heinemann, 1958)
*The Unknown Ajax* (William Heinemann, 1959)
*A Civil Contract* (William Heinemann, 1961)
*The Nonesuch* (William Heinemann, 1962)
*False Colours* (The Bodley Head, 1963)
*Frederica* (The Bodley Head, 1965)

*Black Sheep* (The Bodley Head, 1966)
*Cousin Kate* (The Bodley Head, 1968)
*Charity Girl* (The Bodley Head, 1970)
*Lady of Quality* (The Bodley Head, 1972)

## Historical Novels

*The Great Roxhythe* (Hutchinson, 1922)
*Simon the Coldheart* (William Heinemann, 1925)
*Beauvallet* (William Heinemann, 1929)
*The Conqueror* (William Heinemann, 1931)
*Royal Escape* (William Heinemann, 1938)
*My Lord John* (The Bodley Head, 1975)

## Contemporary Novels

*Instead of the Thorn* (Hutchinson, 1923)
*Helen* (Longmans and Co., 1928)
*Pastel* (Longmans and Co., 1929)
*Barren Corn* (Longmans and Co., 1930)

## Detective Novels

*Footsteps in the Dark* (Longmans and Co., 1932)
*Why Shoot a Butler?* (Longmans and Co., 1933)
*The Unfinished Clue* (Longmans and Co., 1934)
*Death in the Stocks* (Longmans and Co., 1935)
*Behold, Here's Poison* (Hodder & Stoughton, 1936)
*They Found Him Dead* (Hodder & Stoughton, 1937)
*A Blunt Instrument* (Hodder & Stoughton, 1938)
*No Wind of Blame* (Hodder & Stoughton, 1939)
*Envious Casca* (Hodder & Stoughton, 1941)
*Penhallow* (William Heinemann, 1942)
*Duplicate Death* (William Heinemann, 1951)
*Detection Unlimited* (William Heinemann, 1953)

## Short Story Collections

*Pistols for Two* (William Heinemann, 1960)
*Snowdrift* (William Heinemann, 2016)